AS
A Framework for Application Management

ASL
A Framework for Application Management

Remko van der Pols

Title: ASL A Framework for Application Management
Author: Remko van der Pols

Translation from Dutch: Hans van Bemmelen
Review board: Machteld Meijer, Brian Johnson, Dick Costeris, Bert Franken
Project management: BMG
Cover design: DTPresto grafisch ontwerp & layout
Layout and typesetting: BEELDVORM, Pijnacker
Print: Hentenaar Boek

Publisher: Van Haren Publishing (info@vanharen.net)

Edition: First print, first edition, January 2004
ISBN: 90 77212 05 1

© ASL Foundation/Van Haren Publishing 2004

All rights reserved. No part of this publication may be reproduced, stored in a retrieval system, or transmitted in any form or by any means, electronic, mechanical, photocopying, recording or otherwise, without the prior permission in writing of the publisher.

Preface

Information systems have been developed, managed and maintained for decades. Every application management organisation has developed its own way of working and so far little effort has been made to standardise the maintenance and control of the application management processes. This is surprising given that application management accounts for a large proportion of IT expenditure. Standard work processes will generally lead to cost reductions. As it is expensive to reinvent the wheel it is better to benefit from the experiences of others.

Fortunately, the tide is turning and there is now an effective option for application management. This has resulted in a process framework and underlying best practices for application management (i.e. maintenance and control, enhancement and renovation of applications). This framework is called ASL (Application Services Library) and is the only public domain application management standard in the world. The framework includes all processes needed to deliver a comprehensive application management service and has been available for several years.

In this book Remko van der Pols gives a clear description of the Application Services Library framework and provides the first in-depth description of the application management processes. He has done an excellent job and clearly positions the ASL processes as complementary to the Information Technology Infrastructure Library (ITIL). He also identifies options to improve the provision of IT services as a whole. He was greatly supported by colleagues such as Machteld Meijer-Veldman, one of the architects of ASL. Some of the extensive ASL experience built up by PinkRoccade was incorporated into the framework by Chris Nap, Kees Deurloo, Dolf Hoogland, Frank van Outvorst, René Sieders and Leo Plucinski. The assessors were René Visser and, of course, Pieter Hofman, the brains behind R2C, an earlier model on which parts of ASL are based.

As the Application Services Library is in the public domain, both internal as external IT service providers can benefit from the standardisation of the application management processes through uniform and unambiguous communications. There are very clear opportunities for gains through a combination of cost reduction and quality improvement. The ASL Foundation will promote ASL as the de facto standard for application management through publicity, quality assurance and a knowledge database.
You will find more information on www.aslfoundation.org or you may contact us on info@aslfoundation.org.

I would like to thank everybody who has contributed to the translation of this reference work, especially the review board Machteld Meijer-Veldman, Brian Johnson, Bert Franken and Dick Costeris and Herbert Boland, the project manager.

I hope that you will become as inspired by ASL as many before you and that you will be able to benefit from it.

Bilthoven, January 2004
Gert J. van Heun
Managing director ASL Foundation

Contents

	Preface 5
CHAPTER 1	*Introduction* *9*
	1.1 Background 9
	1.2 Objective 11
	1.3 Structure 11
CHAPTER 2	*ASL position and messages* *13*
	2.1 The application management environment 13
	2.2 The ASL messages 14
	2.2.1 Application management requirements 14
	2.2.2 The single point of contact: the service team 15
	2.2.3 Clear agreements: service level agreements 16
	2.2.4 Looking towards the future: proactive IT support ... 18
	2.2.5 Public domain 20
CHAPTER 3	*The ASL framework* *21*
	3.1 Application management framework 21
	3.2 The structure of the ASL framework 23
	3.2.1 Services approach and applications approach 23
	3.2.2 Strategy, management and operations 24
CHAPTER 4	*The maintenance processes* *27*
	4.1 Introduction 27
	4.2 Incident management 29
	4.3 Configuration management 34
	4.4 Availability management 38
	4.5 Capacity management 43
	4.6 Continuity management 47
CHAPTER 5	*Enhancement and renovation* *53*
	5.1 Introduction 53
	5.2 Impact analysis 55
	5.3 Design 60
	5.4 Realisation 64
	5.5 Testing 68
	5.6 Implementation 72

CHAPTER 6 *Connecting processes* 77
    6.1 Introduction 77
    6.2 Change management 78
    6.3 Software control and distribution 81

CHAPTER 7 *Management processes* 87
    7.1 Introduction 87
    7.2 Planning and control 90
    7.3 Cost management 95
    7.4 Quality management 99
    7.5 Service level management 103

CHAPTER 8 *Applications Cycle Management (ACM)* 109
    8.1 Introduction 109
    8.2 ICT developments strategy 112
    8.3 Customer environment strategy 115
    8.4 Customer organisation strategy 117
    8.5 Life cycle management 120
    8.6 ICT portfolio management 123

CHAPTER 9 *Organisation Cycle Management (OCM)* 127
    9.1 Introduction 127
    9.2 Market definition 132
    9.3 Account definition 135
    9.4 Skills definition 137
    9.5 Technology definition 141
    9.6 Service delivery definition 143

CHAPTER 10 *Relationships with other forms of management* 147
    10.1 Introduction 147
    10.2 Why have ASL in addition to the other management models? ... 147
    10.3 Process interfaces 150
    10.4 The service team and its structure 153

CHAPTER 11 *Application and introduction of ASL* 159
    11.1 Applying the ASL framework 160
    11.2 Initial state 161
    11.3 Implementing ASL 161
    11.4 The end result 162

APPENDIX 1 *ASL processes* 165
APPENDIX 2 *Notes to the process flowcharts* 167
APPENDIX 3 *Further reading* 169
APPENDIX 4 *ASL Foundation* 171

CHAPTER 1

Introduction

ASL is the acronym of Application Services Library; a collection of best practice guidance about managing application development and maintenance. There are four key messages:
— Application management, the maintenance and enhancement of Information Systems, is becoming increasingly important.
— The market demands that application management becomes more professional and more forward looking, this is partly a result of the developments in infrastructure management (technical management).
— There are no standard management processes, the best practices differ between organisations and systems.
— There is now a generic framework for application management: Application Services Library (ASL).

1.1 Background

The ever-increasing role of application management
Information systems have been managed, maintained and enhanced for over three decades. Together, these activities are known as application management, and are probably the most common job in the IT industry. The focus is usually on the development of information systems, and rarely on their maintenance and enhancement (management and updating). However, organisations are not interested in the development of information systems for their own sake – they want to use and modify such systems to support their operations.

The role of effective applications and application management will increase in the next few years. Increasing connectivity will not reduce the need for information systems and their effective maintenance and enhancement – on the contrary, their performance, good or bad, will only become more apparent. The increasing need for flexibility and a shorter time-to-market means that applications and their components will have a longer life, simply because there is no time to replace them. Finally, now that information technology has been used for forty years, the demand is for replacement of existing systems, rather than introducing more information technology. The new applications will simply replace the old ones.

There is a demand for more professional application management
Application management is essential because the operation of the business processes depends on it. In recent years, interest in application management has increased significantly. The introduction of ITIL greatly encouraged a service-based approach. However, ITIL is primarily concerned with infrastructure. So far there has been no public domain methodology for application maintenance and enhancement.

The lack of uniformity
Another development is the greater differentiation in application management and the demands made of it. The technical developments of the last thirty years are reflected in application management: the transition from large legacy systems (with strict requirements in terms of stability, reliability and security) to the new legacy of client-server systems and finally dynamic systems based on the Internet (the future legacy). All of these require application management, and to add to the complexity, there are more dependencies than ever before. This means that application management cannot depend on a single standard solution, or one set of best practices. Instead, it demands a framework which is filled with best practices to suit each situation.

ASL
All these needs are met by ASL. ASL is a framework for application management processes. It is the public domain standard for application management. It is an independent standard, separate from the IT Infrastructure Library (ITIL), but linked to it in terms of adherence to standards for managing processes and providing a coherent, rigorous, public domain set of guidance. The reason for this is that infrastructure management is different from application management. Another aspect is that flexible business operations do not require large organisations or processes, but instead small, complete units. ASL ties in with all these developments.

ASL is more than just a framework. It is supported by best practices drawn from a number of organisations (see www.aslfoundation.org). The ASL concept is continually being developed by the foundation and its supporters.

This book introduces ASL and its philosophy for the maintenance and enhancement of applications. Please note that elsewhere the ASL concepts of 'maintenance and enhancement' are sometimes referred to as 'management and updating'.
It also includes a thorough discussion of the framework. The processes relevant to maintenance and management are discussed on the basis of practical expertise, and the practical approach extends to the examples and subjects covered. These processes set the di-

rection which ensures that an organisation will be able to operate effectively in the market in the medium term, as there are now very few organisations which are not dependent on information systems.

1.2 Objective

The requests for this book came from different backgrounds. The objectives of this book are to provide:
- information about the background and objectives of ASL;
- a structure for setting up ASL processes and links to the associated best practices;
- a convenient reference book about the processes.

This book will therefore help you learn:
- more about the ASL framework and the links to the associated practices;
- more about the maintenance and enhancement of information systems;
- how to organise these activities, and what needs to be considered.

This book does not provide:
- ASL as a whole, the best practices: those are available from the ASL Foundation;
- a step-by-step manual for maintenance, enhancement and renovation – after all, application management is not something you can just learn from a book.

1.3 Structure

The structure of this book is as follows: Chapter 2 discusses the environment surrounding ASL, such as the trends, the requirements ASL aims to meet, and the major concepts. Chapter 3 discusses the general ASL framework: the structure of the model in outline, as well as the resulting clusters of ASL processes.

The following chapters develop these clusters and the underlying processes in greater detail using a standard structure, starting with an introduction of the objective of the process, followed by a description of the major issues relevant to the process, then the process activities, results and relationships with other processes. The first two sections of these chapters provide background and some details about ASL. The last three sections of these chapters about each process (activities, results and relationships) are highly detailed and provide the reference element of this book.

Chapter 10 discusses the position of ASL in its environment and how it fits into it, as well as the detailed relationships between ASL and other models such as the Functional Management model and ITIL. The implementation of ASL is discussed in Chapter 11.

CHAPTER 2

ASL position and messages

> **The ASL messages**
> — Application management does not operate in a vacuum, it forms the bridge between functional management (the client) and technical management (the computer centre).
> — The requirements associated with application management include uniformity, control, reliability, clear structure, and an eye to the future.
> — ASL presents these messages through the service team, service levels and associated customer units, the public domain approach, and processes for the applications and application management organisation which are ready for future challenges.

2.1 The application management environment

Application management does not operate in a vacuum, it has links with other forms of management: functional management and technical management. These forms of management were identified by M. Looijen in *Information systems, Management, Control and Maintenance*, see Figure 1. This structure is also used in Thiadens' lectures and books, but the naming of the management disciplines and processes is still being discussed within the Netherlands. However, despite the ongoing terminology discussions, these elements are now widely recognised.

Functional management is responsible for maintaining the functionality of an ICT resource, on behalf of the user organisation. In essence, functional management acts as the owner who commissions the information system.

Application management is responsible for maintaining and enhancing the application software and databases. This means that it manages and maintains the information system (application). This requires expertise in areas such as programming, systems development, design and impact analysis.

Technical management is responsible for maintaining the operations of the information system, consisting of the hardware, software and databases. In essence, it is the organisation which runs the information systems and maintains the infrastructure. This will often be the computer centre. ITIL is a widely adopted standard in this area.

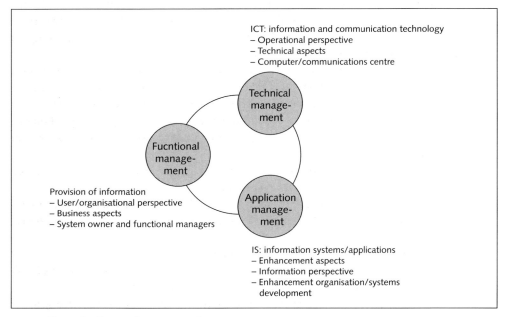

Figure 1   Forms of management

As its name suggests, ASL is only concerned with the second form of management: application management.

2.2   The ASL messages

2.2.1   Application management requirements

The development of ASL was based on a number of requirements and developments. It also benefited from the strengths of other management models. This led to the identification of the requirements to be met by ASL, which include:
- *Transparency*, organisations have a great need for clear information about application management services and the associated costs. Given the magnitude of these costs they have to be in-line with market rates.

- *Management* of costs, applications and the provision of services. Clearly, transparency is useless if there is no management. In many organisations, the need for applications is linked to the primary business processes. This requires careful consideration, valid basis, and comparison of the alternatives (business case).
- *Transferability and compatibility* of people and the application management organisation. The provision of information is essential to many businesses – without effective information systems there is no business. The continuity of information systems is therefore essential to the continuity of the organisation. Dependence on a few individuals (designers or programmers) is incompatible with that.
- *Flexibility* of applications and a forward-looking approach. Information systems are now so large that their replacement often takes years. Many applications have a longer life than expected. Around 80% of the current applications will still be in use in five years. As applications are at the core of the organisation they affect the competitive position of a business, now and in five years. It would therefore be appropriate to take a longer term approach to these information systems.
- *Reliability*, an inadequate information system poses an immediate, major risk to the continuity of an information-intensive organisation.
- *Uniformity* of application management and compatibility between applications are increasingly important given the explosive growth in connectivity between organisations.

ASL has four main concepts to meet these requirements:
- The service team concept: providing a central point of contact which is responsible for all ICT services, to present a uniform interface to the user organisation.
- Service levels: as a tool for managing the provision of services, as well as providing information about the costs.
- Proactive innovation of applications and services.
- The public domain concept.

2.2.2 The single point of contact: the service team

ASL assumes that there is one body, the *service team* which is responsible for managing the entire life cycle of the provision of information. It serves as a bridge between the user organisation and the IT professionals, and provides a clear point of contact for the customer.

A service team makes the ICT organisation transparent to the customer. There is one body responsible for the operation, maintenance and updating of their information supply. The service team operates as a partner of the user organisation, and as the IT services contractor.

A service team provides a single point of contact for all organisations required to provide the information supply service as a whole. Hence the service team may represent more

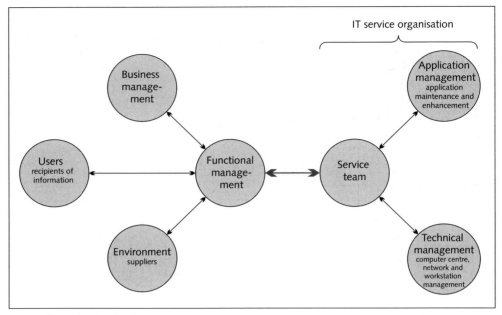

Figure 2 Service team

than one organisation. There should be long-term agreements about development, use and operation. This cooperation is illustrated in Figure 2. The service team interacts mainly with functional management. The service team is responsible for the overall quality of the provision of information, service levels, and service level monitoring and reporting.

A user organisation may liaise with more than one service team. Similarly, a technical management organisation and an application management organisation can operate in more than one service team. A service team operates as an entity, with a clearly defined customer and comparable service requirements. This will be discussed in greater detail in Chapter 10.

2.2.3 Clear agreements: service level agreements

Service levels
Services can only be provided professionally if somebody is accountable for the results. Consequently, there should be agreements for each product where the contractor undertakes to meet these agreements. In ASL, this responsibility is defined in terms of service levels. The objective of these agreements is that the client and users can understand, verify and manage the ICT services. The combination of services, products and performance criteria which the contractor undertakes to provide is defined in the form of a *service level*

agreement (SLA). A SLA defines the obligations and responsibilities of the parties providing and using the services. The underlying principle is that the current and future needs of the customer are met at a reasonable cost. A SLA includes guarantees for the provision of services, and criteria to measure the quality of the provision of services.

These criteria are defined by the service team in consultation with the business manager and the system owner. Where possible they should be defined in units which the business manager and end users can recognise and manage. This contributes to the negotiations about the quality and quantity of the services to be provided, and the associated costs. It results in a customer/supplier relationship through which business managers can effectively direct the providers of ICT services, particularly in terms of output.

Service level agreements make it possible to measure, control and manage ICT services. Furthermore, agreements are also made about the way in which the user organisation and ICT service provider will cooperate. These agreements and procedures lend structure to the cooperation and have a major impact on the perceived service quality.

Transparent costs
Agreements alone are not enough. An effective comparison of the service provided and the associated performance, service level and costs requires clear information about the costs. Thus, the service team defines how the costs are charged for the products and services defined in the SLAs. An essential requirement is that the costs are verifiable and predictable.

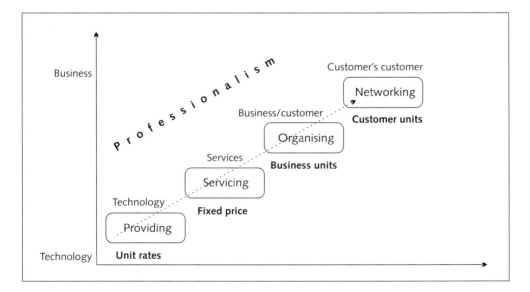

Figure 3   From costs to quality to business value

Appropriate cost units
Where possible, the cost units should be meaningful to the customer. They should be defined in functional terms, in units related to the primary process. There are several options for this. Examples include charges based on the number of units processed by the system, such as salary slips or mortgages. For enhancement there could be a fixed price for each release or functional item, or the charges could be based on the effect experienced by the customer.

For example, an ICT partner could be paid in accordance with the reduction of the cycle times. This charging regime means that the service team, as the ICT partner, shares the business risks of the customer. Thus the ICT supplier will benefit directly from smoothly operating business processes.

	Technology	**Services**	**Business focus**	**Environment focus**
Focus	On technology	On the provision of services	On the business process of the customer organisation	On the environment of the customer organisation and the customer's customers
Service	Providing personnel	Providing services	Acting as a partner	Acting as a clearing house
Management focus	Quantity	Quality Process structure Metrics	Flexibility Effectiveness Efficiency	Innovation Added value Social responsibility
Billing	Unit costs	Fixed price	Business units	Customer units
Step to the next stage	Process structure	Customer focus	Globalisation	?

2.2.4 Looking towards the future: proactive IT support

The responsibility for ICT support is not linked to the lifespan of the systems, but to that of the processes within the customer organisation. Experience shows that applications have a much longer lifespan than expected. The market is slowly moving to a situation in which existing and new applications overlap. Anticipating developments in a timely fashion prevents wasted investments and promotes continuous support. A business manager not only expects to get an acceptable level of service at acceptable cost in the near future, but is also interested in the situation in the next three to five years. This means that *life cycle management* is required. Hence, the efforts should not only aim to support, facilitate and stimulate the customer's current business processes, but also the

future processes. This has two consequences for the application management organisation:
- It has to consider the future of the applications it maintains for its customers.
- It has to decide if the current services and quality criteria will still be appropriate for its customers and users in a few years' time.

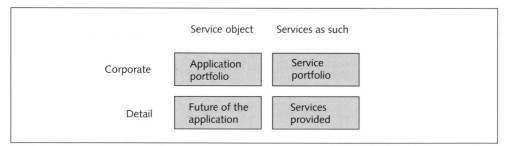

Figure 4 Issues to be considered for the future

Application renovation
The regular evaluation of developments in the environment and in the user organisation, and anticipating these developments, provides a long-term perspective for the applications. This perspective is reflected in the active support of the application portfolio and innovation strategies. An innovation strategy should be based on an analysis of the current ICT situation, the expected developments affecting the customer and its environment, and developments in ICT. An analysis of these factors can be used to outline the future ICT infrastructure. This results in the continuous and planned replacement of the ICT infrastructure as a whole, to safeguard the quality and continuity of the provision of information. Inappropriate investments are avoided as ICT investments can be assessed on the basis of the requirements contained in the outline. Renovation is not limited to isolated information systems, instead it also addresses the applications as a whole (application portfolio).

Service renovation
Anyone providing ICT services should not only consider the future application portfolio of their existing customers, but also develop a strategy for the services to be provided in the medium term. This should not be limited to the services as a whole, but also extend to the individual level (customer or system). The services offered by application management organisations are often reactive or even restrict the customer requirements. This applies to the range of services as a whole as well as to the service provided in terms of the maintenance and enhancement of isolated applications.

This issue is still current, even in the climate of professionalism and SLAs. A common joke is that a service level is just a new way of the ICT organisation saying that something is impossible. Practical experience shows that the introduction of maintenance and enhancement processes often leads to an application management organisation which is professional, but also rigid. A regular review at the strategic level will ensure that ICT providers not only do things right, but also keep doing the right things.

2.2.5 Public domain

A clear trend in ICT is to integrate applications across organisations. The Internet has made it possible to connect information systems across organisations. Consequently, there are now chains of connected information systems. This means that the application management and application management organisations of different entities are suddenly linked and become dependent on each other. Hence the need for uniform communications is rapidly increasing. This is one of the principal reasons for creating ASL in the public domain. The ASL concepts and best practices are managed by a foundation in which several large organisations are represented. The aim of the foundation is to update and improve the best practices, introduce new best practices, update the framework, and ensure that it is compatible with the developments in the real world. ASL should not be a static entity which leads to a number of dialects. Instead, the expertise and experience of the organisations which use it should provide feedback to ASL. This will contribute to ASL users being part of a knowledge organisation.

CHAPTER 3
The ASL framework

The ASL messages
— To be proactive and accountable for its results, an application management organisation has to undertake operational, management and strategic processes.
— The operational and management processes monitor stability, continuity and compatibility with the customer's business processes. The strategic processes set the direction in the long-term.
— Application management is based on a focus on service combined with a thorough knowledge of the customer's processes.

This chapter introduces the ASL framework by discussing the different aspects of ASL which underlie the structure of the framework. The elements of the framework are discussed first, followed by the structure of the framework.

3.1 Application management framework

The ASL framework comprises six clusters of processes, as shown in Figure 5.

Maintenance
There are three process clusters at the operational level. Firstly, there is the *maintenance* cluster within application management. It aims to ensure that the current applications are used in the most effective way to support the business processes, using a minimum of resources, and leading to a minimum of operational interruptions. The primary objective of application management is that applications offer this support.

Enhancement/renovation
The next cluster is that of *enhancement/renovation*. The objective of these processes is to ensure that the applications are modified in-line with the changing requirements which result from changes in the process and the environment. Thus, applications should con-

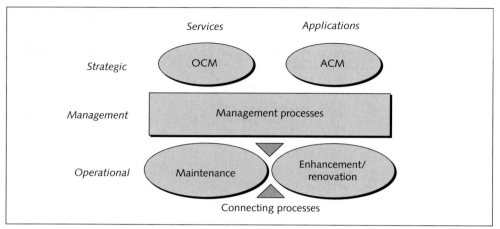

Figure 5 ASL model

tinue to support the business process effectively in the near future. These processes provide modifications to the software, documentation and data models of the applications.

Connecting processes
The above process clusters are not independent, they are closely related as they apply to the same application objects. Software and data are transferred from enhancement to maintenance. Consequently, synchronisation and coordination are essential. For this reason there are two processes to provide coordination.

Management processes
The *management processes* cluster ensures that all of the above process clusters are managed as a whole. This management covers both the service and enhancement aspects. The objective of this cluster is to ensure that the existing activities are implemented in accordance with the objectives, agreements and chosen strategy.

Applications Cycle Management – ACM
The ACM cluster aims to develop a long-term strategy for the information supply objects as well as the information supply of an organisation as a whole, in-line with the long-term strategies of the organisation.

Organisation Cycle Management – OCM
In this era of increasing flexibility the application management organisation cannot expect to provide application management for a number of applications in perpetuity. The user organisation may choose another supplier, even if the application management organisation is an in-house service. This means that there are two aspects to be considered:

the future of the information supply (applications), and the future of the application management organisation.

Once these aspects have been separated, the best policies can be set for each of them. This means that strategic decisions bout the future of the information supply (e.g. ASP, ERP, etc.) are separated from the skills and strategies of the supplier.

The OCM cluster aims to ensure that the strategies and future of the service organisation are developed. It outlines the future of the service organisation (i.e. the application management organisation), and develops the strategies.

Process cluster	Focus	Scope	Time consideration	Nature
Operational and connecting processes	Now	Large	Continuous	Operational
Management processes	Now and the coming year	Small	Continuous	Tactical
Strategic processes	Next few years	Small	Regular	Strategic

Figure 6 Process clusters

3.2 The structure of the ASL framework

The ASL framework uses two criteria to form clusters of application management processes, which will be discussed below. These are:
1. The distinction between service processes and applications. The applications approach is distinct from other forms of management, such as technical management.
2. The distinction between strategic (policy setting), management and operational processes.

3.2.1 Services approach and applications approach

The first criterion requires further explanation. Under the ASL philosophy, application management refers to the support of business processes by information systems, for the lifetime of those business processes. This includes two approaches:
1. *Supporting* the business processes: keeping the applications running (the traditional management aspect). This means providing an uninterrupted service. Key issues include continuity, up-time, etc. The emphasis lies on the services which are provided and which make it possible (together with technical or infrastructure management) to use the applications. This aspect amounts to around 10 to 20% of application management as a whole.
2. For the lifetime of the *business processes*. Organisations evolve, and environments and markets change. The supporting information systems also have to change to continue to provide the best possible support in future. In this cluster of processes the key issue is the

updating of applications to meet future requirements. The expertise is specific to the application. This aspect normally amounts to the largest part of application management.

In practice, the distinction between these two approaches is readily apparent in organisations.

Services approach
The true objective of application management is to ensure that the applications which have been developed are made available to the users in the organisation. This aspect is clearly focussed on the services. The same applies to the future of the application management organisation, i.e. the services to be provided in future and the requirements associated with them. This services approach is aimed at providing services to individuals or organisations.

Applications approach
Applications support the business processes of organisations, and are often incorporated in them. To ensure that the applications will continue to be provided in the future, they have to change in-line with the business processes of the user organisation. This means that application management requires a thorough familiarity with the business processes of the user organisation, their customers, developments in this area, and the applications themselves.

The application processes are largely substantive. Many methods have been developed for the structured implementation of these processes, to support and shape the substantive elements. Examples are the steps involved in making a design, diagramming techniques, division into stages, models, types of documentation, etc. These substantive elements are not covered by ASL as it does not provide standards for these aspects but allows an organisation to choose an appropriate option, such as DSDM, Yourdon, SSADM, structured programming, OOD, etc.

3.2.2 Strategy, management and operations

The ASL processes are divided into three levels:
- operational;
- management;
- strategic.

Operational processes
The operational processes are clearly the most important and therefore at the top of the list, they form the objective of an application management organisation. Under the ASL philosophy 'operational' does not just mean carrying out basic activities: any organisation with responsible and highly trained personnel should exhibit a high level of self-direction and learning ability.

Chapter 3 The ASL framework

Management processes
The management processes fit in between the operational and strategic processes – they provide the link between strategy and operations.

Strategic processes
A number of processes set the policies, to define the strategy of the organisation. Initially, it is essential to take a step back from the existing structures and methods, instead considering the future in its essentials, and choosing a direction based on the developments. Under the ASL philosophy this is not done constantly but once every year or every other year. It requires a structured look at the current situation and external developments, identifying the objectives, verifying their feasibility, and then defining the strategy accordingly. These clusters of processes are discussed in greater detail in the following chapters.

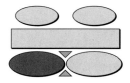

CHAPTER 4

The maintenance processes

The ASL messages
— Using applications requires separate maintenance processes within application management.
— These processes are similar to the ITIL processes, but are still part of application management.
— These processes have many interfaces with the ITIL processes with the same names.
— There are few one-to-one relationships. This is because many applications may be running on the infrastructure, and often at several locations.

4.1 Introduction

The objective of the maintenance processes is to ensure that the applications are operated and used in the best possible way to support the business processes, using a minimum of resources and causing the least disruption in the organisation. Operating and using applications requires application-specific expertise, hence there are a number of application management processes which address this area.

The management processes are also included in ITIL, with similar objectives. Of course, the development of these processes in ASL is different, due to the nature of application management. Similarly, the requirements, performance criteria and other aspects can be quite different. This is discussed below. There are also close connections between the processes in terms of the provision of information.

Issues
Information systems are set up to be used, and operated by technical maintenance. The effective operation of applications in the long term requires in-house expertise. The areas relevant to the maintenance of information systems are:
- *Identification* and management of the service objects (*configuration items*).
- *Availability* and reliability of these objects.

- Deployment of the required *capacity* to provide the services effectively.
- Questions, requirements and faults affecting the objects or services (*incidents*).

These areas lead to five closely related processes.

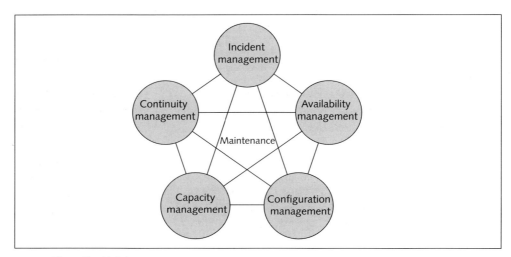

Figure 7 Maintenance processes

The relationship between application management and technical management
The relationship between application management and technical management is one-to-many relationship. Technical management usually runs a number of applications, which are the responsibility of different application management organisations.

Application management organisations may develop information systems (packages or distributed systems) which may run on several information sites. Furthermore, different sites may use different versions of the applications. Consequently, there may be differences in configuration management practices between application management and technical management. For example, configuration management within application management covers many platforms. Configuration management by technical management may cover many different applications from a number of suppliers. The same applies to incident management and certain other issues. This is discussed in greater detail in Chapter 10.

The processes develop in different ways
As mentioned in the preceding section, the relationship between application management and technical management is not a one-to-one relationship. The way in which the processes are developed also differs between the disciplines. Application management translates the business requirements with respect to the information system to a techni-

cal solution which can then be operated by technical management. Here, the translation is one from functionality to technology.

The effective operation of larger systems often requires a knowledge of this form of translation. In turn, this knowledge about the structure of the application, characteristics, internal relationships within the applications and their idiosyncrasies demands a knowledge of IT, system development, programming and design.

Examples:
- A functional manager has an ad hoc information requirement. The application manager will identify the required operations and conditions and may also decide that the operation should not coincide with certain other operations as they use the same data files and might interfere with each other. (This could lead to a deadlock, corrupted data, or extremely long processing times.)
- The functional manager indicates that in the coming year the number of updates of a particular type will double. The application manager knows that the data access method will have to modified to deal adequately with this. Additional indices will be needed, or the internal rows of the program scaled up. This knowledge is application management knowledge, not technical management knowledge. The differences will be addressed in greater details in the discussion of the processes below.

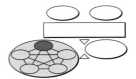

4.2 Incident management

Objective
Incident management is the process which is responsible for the primary response to questions, requests and interruptions, including communications with users and functional management. Thus, this process manages the response to questions and incidents. Consequently it includes many of the activities of a service desk or help desk. This means that incident management plays an important role in meeting service levels. The objectives include ensuring the continuity of services by restoring the agreed service level as soon as possible whenever a deviation is observed, and being available to deal with questions, requests and comments from customers about the current and future services.

Issues
Types of incidents
An *incident* is a question, request, service deviation, etc. with respect to an existing application or its operation. They are generated by technical management, the customer organisation (*calls*) and other application management processes. Typical examples of calls in application management include bug reports, requests for change, requests for ad hoc operations, and questions about applications. The incident management process accepts

these calls and incidents, logs them, and initiates actions to respond to them. This process also monitors their follow-up.

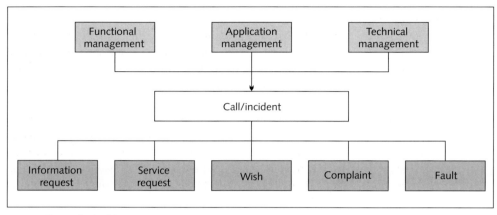

Figure 8   Incident types

Depending on the type of the incident, the scale, number of occurrences, and implications, an incident may be upgraded to a problem.

Problems
A problem is an incident with a legacy. Quite apart from the resolution of the incident, it requires a more extensive investigation to decide if a long-term solution should be developed. A problem is an undesirable situation which cannot be resolved within a single process and which requires a structured analysis and solution. Problems can also be generated by other ASL processes.

Proactive communication
Proactive communication is provided, in addition to reactive communication in response to requirements or complaints. This includes information about changes to applications, changes in the way they are used, and changes in the services to customers (unavailable due to ...). These are also handled by incident management and aim to prevent calls in response to a lack of information.

Responding to problems
Normally, the quality management process will respond to problems. The reason for this is that in application management most of the problems are not identified by incident management (and apparent to users). In most cases, substandard applications, maintenance difficulties or poor performance are not immediately apparent to users (except in terms of enhancement costs and slipping schedules). These faults are normally uncov-

ered by planning and control, testing, implementation or the acceptance test. Normally, new application releases have relatively few bugs when they are commissioned. This means that most of the problems are not reported by incident management.

Responding to incidents
Bugs in applications generally result in a quick improvement to the application, either a patch or a work-around, particularly for bespoke software. Fixing the bug requires a thorough analysis of the documentation, software and data. If the response to the incident is adequate then it is not promoted to problem within ASL.

Users may also have requests for change, which are considered in the change management process. They often have to be processed in between urgent changes in response to legislative changes, etc. Less urgent requests may be unfulfilled for years, often they are included in a future release. It would therefore be inappropriate to use the resolution time as a performance criterion. This is a clear difference between application management and technical management.

Relationship with other incident management processes
The target group of this process depends on the organisational structure: functional management and technical management also have help desks with incident management processes. The different incident management processes require effective coordination. If a service team is used there should be only one primary help desk.

Activities
Proactive communications with users about the current services:
- maintaining contact with the end users or functional managers;
- supporting the use of ICT resources and information systems;
- informing users about the impact of changes to ICT services.

Incident resolution (reactive):
- accepting and logging calls and incidents;
- evaluating the call or incident, classifying it and where necessary allocating it to an agent;
- escalating it to a problem where appropriate;
- resolving calls and incidents;
- providing feedback on the status of calls and incidents;
- closing the calls and incidents.

Incident reporting (reporting and control):
- generating reports and status lists of unresolved calls;
- problems, reporting problems;
- logging the time spent on these issues, etc.;
- meeting service levels, where relevant.

Results
Incident recording and incidents:
- incidents: incident, description, person reporting it, etc.;
- incident status;
- information to other management processes (tier two or second-line incidents): process dealing with it, resolution status, cycle time, etc.;
- information to other incident processes within technical management and functional management (tier two incidents): organisation dealing with it, status, cycle time, etc.

Proactive communications:
- communications about developments affecting the application and services;
- information about changes and the status of the application.

Problems:
- cause (incident);
- with underlying causes which justify escalation to a problem.

Incident reporting:
- progress and use of allocated resources;
- where relevant: service level information, status reports;
- evaluation of the progress of the process, incident reports;
- problems.

Relationships with other processes
The incident management process has many close links with other processes, both in terms of communications and incident resolution.

Functional and technical management
Firstly, there are close links with other forms of incident management within functional management and technical management. There is a need for clear agreements about who is the primary contact for users, and how incident records are exchanged. There should be effective coordination between the various incident management processes. Depending on who is the primary user contact, incidents and incident resolution information for tier two incidents will be transferred between incident management processes. This is discussed in greater detail in Chapter 10.

Management processes
Incident management has close links with the service level management process as we need to be aware of the agreements to be able to decide if they were infringed. Furthermore, there are often agreed service levels for the incident management process: times when incidents can be reported, response times to calls, etc. The operation of the incident management process often greatly affects the users' perception of the quality of the

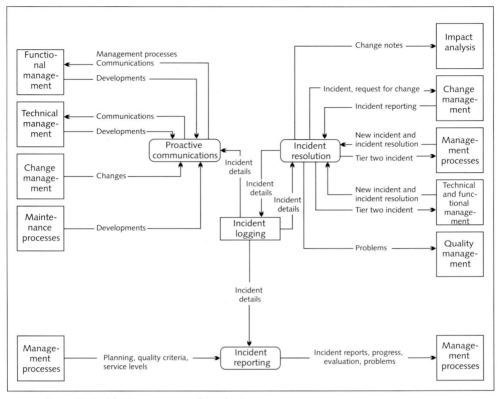

Figure 9 Incident management flow chart

application management organisation. This is another reason why this management information is essential to the service level management process. Furthermore, problems revealed by the incident resolution process form important input for the quality management process. Quality management also provides feedback about problem resolution. Reports are also sent to planning and control about progress, use of resources, and the expected available capacity.

Change management, impact analysis and implementation
The help desk is often the initial point of contact for the customer. Often, reported problems can only be resolved by changes to the application or the application management organisation. Furthermore, changes to the application will impact the users. For this reason, the incident management process has close links with the change management process and other processes. Changes and requests for changes often require further information and an impact analysis. The impact of new releases becomes apparent within the implementation process which provides relevant information to the other management processes.

Maintenance processes
All incidents are reported via the incident management process. All maintenance processes can play a part in solving incidents. However, incident management remains responsible for the incidents. This means that incident management has input relationships with all maintenance processes (the processes generate incidents which are resolved within incident management), as well as output relationships (the maintenance processes provide tier two resolutions and report about them).

4.3 Configuration management

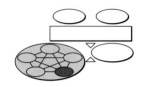

Objective
Configuration management includes the processes which record information about the use of objects (of which there may be different versions) in an information system or application. These records are known as the CMDB (Configuration Management DataBase). The objective of configuration management is to keep records of all application objects, configurations and services which the application management organisation is responsible for, and providing accurate information about these objects to support the other application management processes.

Issues
Application objects
The application objects are the building blocks of the application in a broad sense. They include documentation, programs and source code, data definitions, test files, scripts, etc.

References, not objects
The CMDB does not contain the objects themselves, but references to them (i.e. it is an aid to identification). A CMDB is not a version management system. Instead, it shows which version of an application runs on what platform and where. It is essential for effective application management to know what is used, and where – particularly when distributed systems or packages are used, and when applications may be used in several computer centres. In other words, configuration management concerns the relationships between the technical infrastructure and applications and versions.

There is no need to store all information about all components in the CMDB. However, it is essential that it is possible to determine which version of what object is being used where. This can also be provided by software control and distribution, which keeps track of the relationships between object versions and releases. If the software control is effective then often the release will suffice as a configuration item.

Naming conventions
An application may include a large number of objects: a major information system may well include thousands of programs and hundreds of tables and files. Effective naming conventions are needed to keep track of all this. Normally these conventions cover programs, files and file versions. The conventions often cover more than one system, and they form part of the quality system.

Relationships with technical management
Technical management may also use a configuration database which may include the application objects. It might be possible to use this database. However, particularly when packages and distributed systems are used, the application will run on many platforms and cross the boundaries of technical management organisations. It is also possible that several versions of the same application are used. Under those circumstances the technical management configuration database cannot be used. It is therefore often useful to set up dedicated application management records, containing the details discussed in the previous sections. These records refer to the technical infrastructure. The infrastructure objects are managed by the configuration management process within technical management (hardware, system software, networks, etc.), not by configuration management within application management. However, it will be clear that there is a close relationship.

Service objects
The configuration management process records which application version is used where, and what it comprises. In other words, it records details about the applications defined by service level management in a SLA. The same details can be recorded for the services defined by service level management. These services, specified as service items, can be recorded in a Service Delivery Database (SDDB). The detailed agreements with customers, the service requirements and associated matters are important when responding to incidents. It may therefore be decided to extend this class of objects to include objects concerning application management services, such as service levels, and management and quality plans (project documentation).

Activities
Defining and modifying naming conventions and standards:
- defining naming standards;
- monitoring compliance with the standards;
- extending the standards where appropriate.

Recording configuration times:
- recording and identifying new or existing configuration items;
- monitoring the current status of configuration items and providing information about them;
- providing information for impact analyses (which objects are used where).

Recording service items:
- recording services and service items;
- monitoring the current status of these items.

Providing information:
- providing information about the versions of applications and application objects in use.

Management and reports:
- providing reports about the available objects;
- making time reports, process evaluations, etc.

Results
CMDB:
- application objects (configuration items);
- location where they are used, and additional information such as the contact person, etc.;
- status (version).

SDDB (optional):
- service items;
- service characteristics;
- corresponding documentation (optional).

Naming conventions:
- recognised object types and their naming conventions.

Information about application configurations and their use:
- for impact analysis;
- for incident management;
- reports about the availability of items, and changes.

Relationships
Maintenance processes
Configuration management is a process which provides information to all maintenance processes (e.g. incident management), about what application objects are used where, and what the services include. These information flows were not included in the flow charts, to keep the level of detail manageable.

Software control and distribution
The configuration management process in application management has close relationships with software control and distribution, and configuration management in techni-

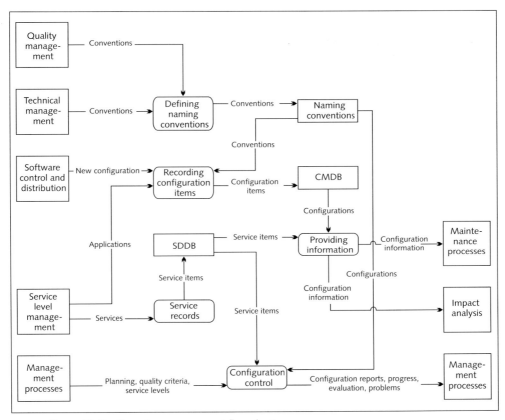

Figure 10 Configuration management flow chart

cal management. The CMDB is the central element in all this. The software control and distribution process covers logistics and object storage (between environments within the enhancement processes), while configuration management covers the current situation in operating environments (which may be diverse). Thus, software control and distribution will regularly transfer new configurations to technical management, and the information about them has to be recorded by configuration management.

In organisations where application management is highly structured, the distinction between software control and distribution and configuration management is sometimes unclear, because the processes and environments are highly integrated. However, it is always possible to distinguish the types of information, information flows, and responsibilities.

Impact analysis
Impact analysis frequently requires information about what application is running where, so that the impact of a change can be determined. Configuration management provides this information to impact analysis.

Management processes
The naming conventions form part of the quality system and are agreed in consultation with technical management. The quality system is the responsibility of the quality management process. Problems concerning configurations and other issues are reported to quality management. The applications in the CMDB, and any services in the SDDB, are specified by service level management. In the context of planning and control, issues such as capacity planning, use of resources, etc. are also relevant.

4.4 Availability management

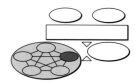

Objective
Availability management includes the processes which provide, monitor and assure the availability of services and application components. The objectives of availability management are:
- ensuring that the applications and services are designed to meet the availability levels demanded by the business;
- providing reports to ensure that the availability and reliability levels are measured and monitored, and fulfil the agreed levels;
- optimising the availability of applications and management with respect to the infrastructure, to deliver cost-effective improvements to the user organisation;
- in the longer term, reducing the number of interruptions and incidents which affect the availability and reliability;
- identifying shortcomings in the availability, and identifying appropriate corrective actions;
- developing an availability plan to ensure that the required measures are implemented so that the reliability and continuity requirements will continue to be met in future.

This means that the reliability management process is not limited to operational aspects. In fact, this applies to all operational processes.

Issues
Availability and reliability are two closely related concepts.

Availability is the extent to which an application item (configuration item) is capable of providing the required functionality at a particular time, or for a particular period of time. This covers starting up and completing (processing or executing) the application, execution in the right order and at the right time, ad hoc jobs, periods when on-line operations are available, and the retention periods of files.

Reliability is the extent to which the object or service provides the agreed or expected functionality, during specified periods. Thus, availability refers to the presence of an object or service, and reliability refers to its correct operation. These quality aspects (see also service level management) relate to the application objects and services.

The *availability of an application* is the extent to which an application or its objects are available for use at the workstation. This relates to the times at which processing can take place, availability of application objects at the required locations (documentation), executing the right operations and specifying their order (e.g. batches at a computer centre), specifying the retention periods of data files at the computer centre (safeguarding mutual dependencies and consistency).

The *reliability of an application* refers to the way in which the application works. Relevant criteria include the number of interruptions when running the application, maximum failure frequency, and the Mean Time Between Failures (MTBF). This is related to issues such as the robustness of the application.

The *availability of a service* refers to the extent to which the application management organisation is available to the user organisation or functional management. Obviously the opening hours of the help desk are an important consideration, but so is whether or not the agreed services defined in the service catalogue (see the service level management process) are provided.

The *reliability of a service* refers to the extent to which the application management organisation fulfils the agreements. Relevant criteria include the Mean Time To Repair (MTTR, the average downtime or time needed to fix a bug or interruption), the time within feedback is given if there is an incident, etc. The quality and maintainability of applications are important elements in this.

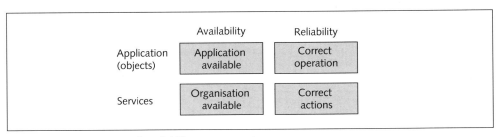

Figure 11 Aspects of availability management

Activities[1]
Developing the availability plan:
- identifying the general requirements (in the service level management and quality management processes) and identifying the routine processing activities;
- identifying special availability requirements (processing deviations or exceptions, ad hoc jobs, etc.);
- verifying the feasibility or impact of modifications to the applications or services, in consultation with the enhancement processes and technical management;
- assessing the impact of new developments (e.g. a new release or new technology) and the reliability and availability;
- identifying and defining the requirements.

Providing the availability, i.e. determining the specifications and measures to realise these objectives:
- requirements and specifications for the necessary infrastructure and functionality;
- defining the requirements (service levels) for subcontractors (e.g. technical management or network providers);
- defining the times at which maintenance, enhancement and upgrading activities can be carried out on the application and infrastructure (e.g. backups).

Availability monitoring, i.e. monitoring the effectiveness of the measures and availability and reliability:
- measuring the availability or reliability of the data processing activities or services, checking if scheduled or ad hoc jobs were indeed executed and completed without faults, or if the applications are/were on-line;
- comparison of the actual figures and the requirements (e.g. using the production schedule);
- making improvements and determining required measures;
- where appropriate: communicating with incident management.

Availability management (reporting and management):
- various availability and reliability reports;
- schedules/planning, progress, time commitment, etc.

Results
Availability and reliability plan:
- detailed availability and reliability requirements (for processing jobs, etc.);
- reliability and availability experience(fault records);

---

[1] Although the names of the activities do not include the term 'reliability' they do address this issue.

Chapter 4 The maintenance processes

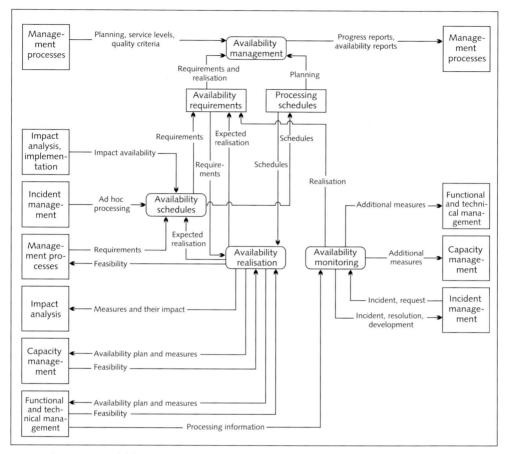

Figure 12 Availability management flowchart

- feasibility of the availability and reliability requirements;
- requirements and measures for technical management, enhancement and functional management.

Processing schedules (planning):
- application production schedule and related information;
- non-standard jobs (ad hoc jobs);
- additional or modified jobs (implementation).

Availability reports:
- progress and planning/schedules;
- availability and reliability reports (availability rates, deviations from the SLA, MTBF, etc.)

Relationships
Incident management
Functional management requests ad hoc jobs which are often routed through incident management. Incident management also receives reports about the availability and reliability of the application, which need to be followed up. (This information may come from technical management, functional management or the users.) The incident management process routes these tier two incidents to the availability management process. However, incident management has the process responsibility for the follow-up of the incident.

Furthermore, application management may report incidents to incident management. Capacity management information may be used for revising schedules, etc.

Other maintenance processes
There are links between the availability management, capacity management and continuity management processes. The measures taken by availability and continuity management often require additional capacity.

Impact analysis and implementation
The impact analysis aims to determine the impact of changes to the information system. The issues considered include reliability and availability. That means that this process provides information about the change. The effect of the change on the availability and reliability, and any required measures is then routed back to the impact analysis.

The implementation of a new release may lead to changes in the production schedules (see preceding item). A new release may also change the cycle times and other physical aspects. These changes should have been communicated during the impact analysis.

Functional and technical management
The applications are executed by technical management. Thus, information about the required processing dates, ad hoc jobs, requirement levels, etc. must be provided to technical management. Technical management then provides information about the completion (results of the processing operations in terms of reliability and availability). Technical management and capacity management also exchange information about the effects of possible measures.

Additional measures to realise the requirements may be proposed to functional management (directly or through incident management).

Management processes
The standard and overall availability and reliability requirements are generated by the service level management and quality management processes. Their feasibility and implementation (measures) are reported (feasibility reports). These processes are also informed about the operations (availability reports). Any long-term problems or requirements in terms of enhancement and renovation are relayed to quality management. Ad-

ditionally, information about planning and progress is provided to planning and control.

4.5 Capacity management

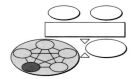

Objective
Capacity management aims to ensure the best possible use of the resources, i.e. at the right place, at the right time, in the right quantity, and at justifiable cost. The objective of capacity management is to allocate the appropriate resources at the right time to the services for the management, use and operation of the system, to ensure that the capacity is used cost-effectively, and will continue to be so in terms of the future needs of the organisation.

Issues
Capacity planning
Capacity management starts with capacity planning. Capacity planning includes determining the demand from the environment, determining the required resource capacity, and identifying and allocating the resources to meet the demand. Personnel planning for management processes is included under planning and control. The following information is needed for capacity planning:
- Data processing volume addressed to the system (number of data updates, etc.) and how the applications operate on this volume.
- Developments in terms of data processing or infrastructure which will affect the capacity use. Examples: a new release with significantly more complex calculations resulting in longer cycle times, or a new release of a database management system which reduces transaction times.

Capacity realisation
Once these requirements have been identified, it is assessed to what extent they can be realised. This analysis is used to take measures (capacity realisation), in consultation with functional and technical management. These analyses propose or implement measures to obtain the required performance. Examples of technical and other measures include:
- Changing the *workload*: changing or shifting the demand. This can be done by shifting processing operations (bearing in mind their interdependencies), dividing operations, not running ad hoc jobs or other jobs.
- Changing the *resources*: increasing (or decreasing or downsizing) the capacity such as adding infrastructure (memory expansion), deploying a faster infrastructure (processor, storage media, etc.), distributing processing over several servers.

- Changing or optimising the *performance*. The options for this include tuning (optimising the deployment of resources and processing in programs and files), de-normalisation (controlled redundancy), deleting data and files (transferring data to archives or deleting unused information from files and databases), access analysis (optimising data access by creating or modifying access paths and indexes used to access data), making program queues larger, storing data or intermediate results differently, etc.

Capacity monitoring
Capacity monitoring includes three activities:
- demand management;
- supply or resource management;
- measuring and monitoring the results: performance management.

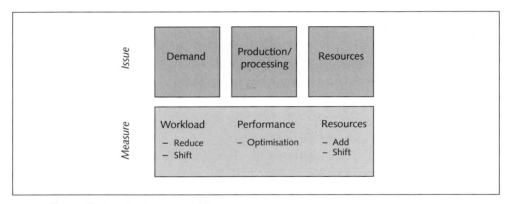

Figure 13 Capacity management issues

Workload management aims to monitor developments in the environment around the system and provide information about it (e.g. volume of data and number of users). This is used to identify trends (e.g. continuing increases in the application data volume). Corrective action is taken where appropriate.

Resource management aims to provide information about the infrastructure and application resources (through configuration management) and any changes in them which affect the capacity. Information from resource management and performance management can be used to identify the requirements which applications and packages impose on the infrastructure.

Performance management aims to monitor the results of running applications, identify trends, and make recommendations to improve the performance. Performance management provides information about the behaviour of applications with different data volumes or changes in functionality. Effective performance management predicts how applications will behave in the future and makes it possible to take appropriate action. The relevant information is generally provided by technical management: measuring response times, cycle times, CPU load, capacity use, network load.

Activities

Capacity planning:
- identifying requirements;
- performance and capacity developments;
- selecting the right approach to reach the required level.

Capacity realisation:
- planning measures;
- resources measures;
- demand-side measures;
- processing measures.

Capacity monitoring:
- workload management;
- resources management;
- performance management;
- generating and dealing with capacity incidents.

Capacity reporting (management and reporting):
- capacity and utilisation reports;
- time and financial reports and service level realisation reports.

Results

Capacity plan:
- premises (expected demand, expected supply, expected performance);
- objectives to be fulfilled;
- capacity measures, additional capacity measures, measures to improve performance (tuning, optimising access, denormalisation, etc.), demand-side measures (e.g. rescheduling).

Capacity and utilisation reports:
- capacity reports;
- utilisation reports (processing, use of resources such as CPU, cycle time, etc.);
- trends;
- internal reports on time commitments, resolved capacity incidents, etc.

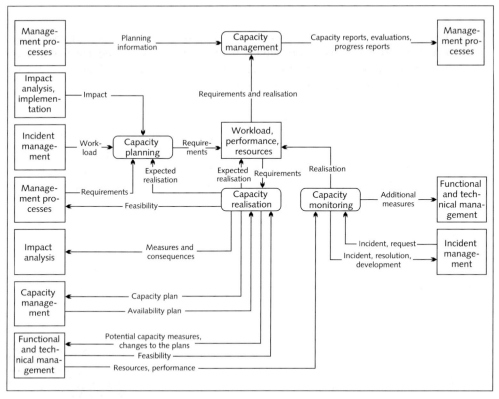

Figure 14 Capacity management flowchart

Relationships
Maintenance processes
Incident management information which is often needed in the capacity management process includes: requests, forecasts and other information about the potential demand, such as the data volume to be processed and busy periods in the organisation. The impact of new releases on the capacity has to be communicated from impact analysis to capacity management, possibly via incident management. The measures required by availability management and continuity management processes often demand additional capacity.

Technical management and configuration management
The configuration management process provides information about where the applications are used. The infrastructure capacity is an important parameter in capacity management. Technical management can deploy additional infrastructure to meet the required service levels. In ASL there are several information flows between capacity management and technical management, such as the processing progress, measures and their feasibility, additional demand, additional capacity, capacity and utilisation reports, etc.

Functional management
Provides information about the expected data volume to be processed, growth in the data volume (e.g. increase in the number of insurance policyholders), etc. Capacity demand peaks can sometimes be reduced by shifting the workload in time. Measures like this have to be coordinated with functional management.

Impact analysis and implementation
The impact analysis aims to determine the effect of changes to the application. This includes the effect on the required capacity. Thus, this process provides information about the changes. The impact of the changes on the required capacity, and any measures required by this, provide feedback for the impact analysis. The actual impact normally becomes clear during the implementation.

Management processes
These cover:
- requirements further to service level management and quality management;
- schedules and revised schedules, etc.;
- capacity measures;
- capacity reports;
- problems, evaluations, etc.

4.6 Continuity management

Objectives
Continuity management refers to all measures taken to ensure the continuity and support of the provision of information (by information systems) in the long term. The objective of continuity management is to ensure the continuity of the business processes by safeguarding the continuity of information systems and taking appropriate measures to ensure the effective operation of the systems (in terms of timeliness and quality), even under exceptional conditions.

Issues
Continuity is the extent to which the information system can operate without interruption (or with an acceptable risk) in the long term. There are a number of potential threats to continuity:
- External threats, from the environment. External hackers may break into an application (unauthorised use). Security measures (information security, physical security, etc.) provide protection against hackers and crackers.
- Internal threats in the form of unauthorised use by insiders. The vulnerability of the system and processing operations to fraud constitute a threat.

- External threats in the form of disruptions due to unforeseen or unavoidable factors (emergencies).
- Internal threats because the resources are no longer supported by suppliers or due to internal resource aspects (e.g. "DOS is well past it", "we no longer have the source code").

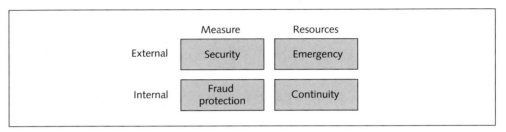

Figure 15 Continuity

Measures

A range of continuity measures can be developed against each of the four threats:

1. *Measures against unauthorised external access.* There are many options for securing the system and infrastructure. Examples include passwords, firewalls and physical security. The options can be assessed through a dependency analysis and vulnerability assessment. In most cases these resources are provided by technical management.
2. *Measures against unauthorised internal access.* Fraud by users or system managers can be prevented by security measures, separating functions (Chinese walls), special authorisations within applications, procedures, audit trails, audit trails of changes to data, securing databases, etc. Internal and external security are closely related. Many of these issues are addressed within applications (e.g. authorisations within applications and audit trails of changes to data).
3. *Measures to protect resources against external threats.* Emergency protection options include back-up facilities (another site where data processing can carry on), secured file back-ups, fire protection, redundant infrastructure and processing resources, etc. Again, most of these resources are provided by technical management. In many cases their utilisation is specified and detailed by application management (see below, under 'Application objects').
4. *Measures to protect resources against internal threats.* Regular and comprehensive assessment of the infrastructure and application resources is an effective option to safeguard their continuity. Appropriate measures include escrow, storage, new releases and migration scenarios.

Application objects

Continuity management tends to be reliant on technical management measures. For example, when considering a back-up site the focus is often on hardware. But when resorting to a back-up site the application objects are also essential. We have to know which executables and data files should be transferred. Simply transferring the executables to the back-up site is not enough. Enhancement will be impossible without the source code. The same applies to documentation. Often, the documentation is only available in hard copy form, with comments scribbled on it and could be lost in a fire. (Of course, this never happens in organisations which have adopted ASL!) The same applies to essential project documentation such as procedures. Protection against unauthorised internal use is often implemented within an application by using separate authorisation procedures, program verification, storing changes instead of overwriting the original data, etc.

Not everything
Providing and testing off-site back-up facilities and security absorbs a lot of funds and energy. Testing all processing operations at a back-up site demands a lot of work and attention. However, it is not always necessary to secure everything, or to have back-up facilities available. Some operations (e.g. infrequent jobs and some reports) are not that time critical. One of the activities in this process is setting priorities and deciding which elements require off-site back-up and which do not.

Don't just design, test
Good intentions often come to nothing. Security measures are not enforced or tested. Most intrusions follow after a hacker simply guesses the password. An off-site back-up test might be unsuccessful because some files are missing, or the wrong versions are used. If the first time the back-up is needed also turns out to be the first test of the arrangements you will have a major problem. In other words, we have to make sure that we actually implement all our good intentions.

Activities
Continuity planning (dependency analysis, vulnerability analysis):
- identify the products and services supplied;
- identify the threats;
- identify the relevance and dependency level;
- undertake the risk assessment;
- determine the desired security, off-site back-up and redundancy levels;
- write the plan.

Continuity realisation (implementing the measures):
- implement the continuity measures (e.g. security, organisational and technical measures, off-site back-up, etc.).

Continuity monitoring:
- test the security measures;
- test the back-ups, roll-backs and off-site back-up facilities;
- test the emergency plan.

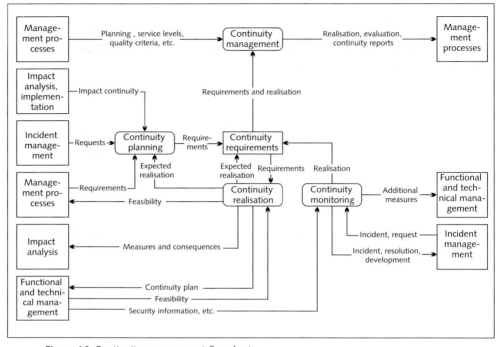

Figure 16 Continuity management flowchart

Results
Continuity plan:
- elements of the dependency and vulnerability analysis, security requirements;
- continuity and security measures in the broadest sense.

Monitoring:
- monitoring and verification programmes;
- continuity reports.

Relationships
Management processes
The framework and outlines of requirements and constraints for continuity are provided by the service level management and quality management processes. They are developed in greater detail in the continuity management process which also assesses their feasibility. The feasibility (dependency and vulnerability analyses and measures) then provides feedback for these processes. The actual realisation, the results of the tests, etc. (continuity reports) provide the input for these processes.

Incident management
The Incident management process routes some incidents to continuity management which has to take measures to resolve the incidents. However, the incident management process continues to monitor the resolution.

Technical management and functional management
The dependency and vulnerability analyses are normally undertaken jointly by technical management and functional management. A range of measures are implemented by technical management or functional management. Much of the basic information for continuity reports is provided by technical management.

Impact analysis and implementation
Impact analysis may require the determination of the effect of changes and releases on the application continuity. The results become apparent during the implementation.

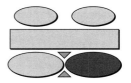

CHAPTER 5

Enhancement and renovation

The ASL messages
— On the whole, enhancement follows the division into stages and processes used for systems development.
— Enhancement has far fewer degrees of freedom and the requirements are stricter: the challenge is to find to best solution within this force field.
— Quality awareness is particularly high in enhancement as any solution which is not perfect keeps coming back. However, there are fewer options for improvement.

5.1 Introduction

The second group of processes includes the enhancement and renovation processes which include impact analysis, design, testing, etc. Enhancement can involve a significant amount of work when major changes are mode or if applications are continuously being improved: this will be done in the form of projects.

Processes
The enhancement processes show the same division used in application development, see Figure 17.

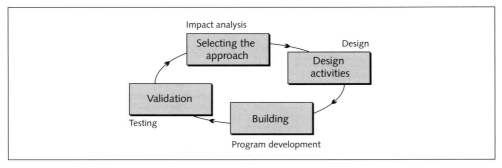

Figure 17 Main elements of enhancement

The processes are shadowed by the live implementation which prepares the environment for the introduction of the solution, i.e. the modified system. Thus, enhancement and renovation includes the following processes:

- *impact analysis:* activities to condition and identify the impact of a request for change;
- *design:* information analysis and design;
- *program development (realisation):* changing, realising and assembling the programs (application objects) into applications;
- *testing:* testing the changed service components, leading to acceptance and sign-off by the customer for the delivered products;
- *live implementation:* final introduction of the changed software and other service components, including conversion, acceptance tests, training, instruction and migration, followed by sign-off.

Differences between development and enhancement

There are some fundamental differences between developing and enhancing applications, although the approach and method are quite similar. Unlike development, maintenance and enhancement are affected by a number of complications:

- *The initial situation is less favourable:* enhancement has to deal with the existing system structure and software. The original reasons for selecting a system structure may be outdated due to changes in the business processes or improved technology. Additionally, continuous enhancement leads to more complex software and structures. The development tools are often outdated and do not provide the modern level of support. During enhancement, developers have fewer options to choose from.
- *The demands are higher:* a new version often has to introduced at a set date. The deadlines are generally firm as legislation takes effect, or because new products have to be intro-

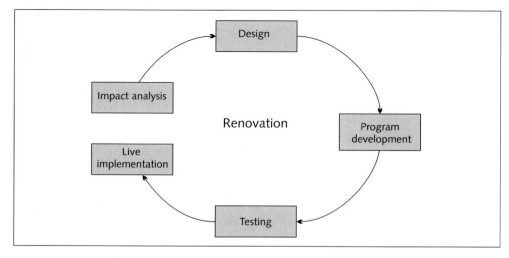

Figure 18 Enhancement and renovation processes

duced onto the market. Furthermore, a new release must operate correctly from the start, in terms of performance and reliability, and the new functionality will be used. When developing new software there is often the option of returning to the older software.
- *The feedback cycle is shorter:* anything less than a perfect solution will soon come back to haunt the designer or builder, it remains part of the application and will have to be considered in the next release.
- *There are fewer options for improvement:* the options for improving the application or its management are more restricted than when developing software as there is often a backlog, there are only limited financial resources, and because management is not aware that improvements lead to a financial return.

These issues always affect enhancement choices and often necessitate compromises. It is rarely possible to introduce a perfect solution. This means that application management has to creatively steer a course between the demand, selected solution and ambitions, feasibility within the constraints, and the risks. These processes are discussed in greater detail below.

5.2 Impact analysis

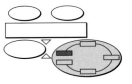

Objective
Impact analysis determines the effect of the proposed changes, which is then used to select the best solution for realising the change. The objective of the process is to effectively and reliably identify the impact in terms of effort, future consequences, use and operation of the proposed changes so that the best solution can be selected. Impact analysis takes a close look at the changes which are combined (and possibly formed into clusters) in the change management process. The impact analysis determines the effects of these changes on the application, the rest of the enhancement and renovation process and the environment. The impact may be higher or lower than originally expected, thus the planning or the content of the releases may be modified in the change management process, further to the outcome of the impact analysis. Hence, these processes often form part of a cycle.

Issues
The impact analysis process is primarily focussed on the application but also considers the following issues, together with the other management disciplines:
- user organisation: which business processes will change, and what is the impact on the customers and users;
- infrastructure: what is the impact of the change on the infrastructure and relevant agreements?

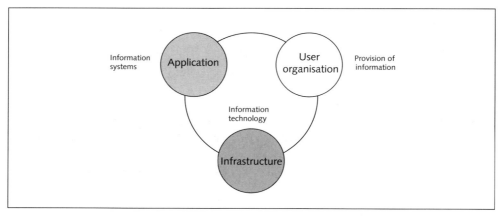

Figure 19 Issues in impact analysis

Application
To identify the impact we had to identify major objects such as functions, subsystems and data which are affected by the changes, and what the relationships between these objects are. This creates a link with the software control and distribution process, which provides the facilities and required information. One of the results of impact analysis is the change set which identifies the application objects which may be modified further to the change. A more detailed descriptions is included in the chapter "Software control and distribution".

Infrastructure
To understand the impact on the infrastructure we have to know where the application runs, and what the potential effect of the changes will be. This information is primarily provided by the maintenance processes. Configuration management is particularly important as it monitors what is used where. However, the information is not only provided by the maintenance processes. If any major changes are planned is advisable to consult the technical management organisation at an early stage.

Users
The impact on the users is determined in consultation with functional management. Because of constraints such as time and capacity, compromises may have to be made in terms of elegance and completeness of the solutions. Furthermore, the user organisation will often have to contribute to the realisation of the change as some activities cannot be automated, or only with great difficulty.

Activities

Defining the change:
- defining the changes to be included in a release (acceptance);
- developing them in greater detail to meet the demand.

Estimating the scale of change:
- identifying the products (configuration items) affected by the planned changes;
- estimating the scale of the modifications to these objects as a result of the proposed change;
- identifying the relationships between the proposed changes and where necessary identifying the relationships with other releases;
- developing a schedule for making and testing these changes.

Estimating the impact:
- estimating the impact on the operating environment, user environment and SLA (required capacity, availability, etc.);
- estimating the long-term impact (enhancement, operation, maintenance, etc);
- identifying any supplementary measures required;
- estimating the risks associated with the changes;
- estimating the scope of the activities associated with the changes and estimating the time required.

Verification and feedback:
- verification with functional management, maintenance processes and technical management;
- feedback to the change management process.

Reporting and control:
- progress monitoring;
- evaluating progress and the process.

Results

Impact analysis report:
- assumptions and premises for the impact analysis;
- definitions of changes and releases;
- impact on objects: affected objects (change set) and impact;
- alternative solution(s);
- activities to be carried out;
- scope and estimate of the human resources required for the releases;
- potential risks and relevant measures;
- impact on user environment, application management and operational environment;
- long-term impact;

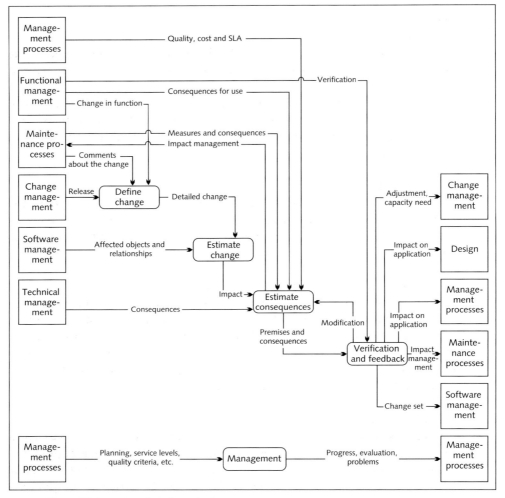

Figure 20 Impact analysis flow chart

- scale of the change (required capacity);
- proposed changes to the release.

Change set:
- affected objects;
- any interaction with other releases.

Progress report:
- schedule, progress;
- and the problems, evaluations.

Relationships
Change management
The impact analysis process is closely linked with the change management process. The change management process identifies the changes which will be made in the relevant releases.

The results of the impact analysis are used to adjust the premises of the change management process. The impact of the change may be so different from what was expected that the definition of the release may have to be modified. This information is then routed to the change management process.

Software control and distribution
The identification of the application objects (programs, documentation, data files) which will have to be modified further to the changes is supported by the software control and distribution process. These objects are also flagged to indicate that they may or will be modified further to a release or change.

Configuration management and technical management
To determine the impact on maintenance and operations we have to identify which applications, or modules or versions of them, are used where. This information is provided by configuration management and can be used to determine the impact of a change on operations. This will involve the other maintenance processes within application management, and technical management. Technical management can also provide information about the operational aspects of a change.

Other maintenance processes
If the processing, availability, required capacity, etc. of the system may be affected then information about the impact is provided to the application management processes, which frequently also provide information about these aspects. Examples of relevant aspects include performance and reliability. To prevent undesirable effects, these processes may also identify additional measures and consequences. The processes provide the mechanism to submit requests for change to incident management. The processes will then provide supporting information for any requests for change.

Design
Design is the next stage following impact analysis. The outcome of the impact analysis provides the primary input for the design process.

Management processes
Impact analysis also provide essential input for the planning and control process. The estimated capacity required for a change will have to be included in this process. Furthermore there will be links with the other management processes if there are additional consequences, for example in terms of the service levels, investments or additional costs,

long-term quality or operational aspects. Of course, these processes take action further to the progress of the impact analysis.

Functional management
When requested, functional management provides additional information about the change. The impact on the user organisation is specified by functional management. Additional information about desirable functional changes is provided by functional management. The impact analysis report is also verified and used for feedback.

5.3 Design

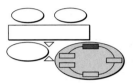

Objective
The objective of the design process is to define and document the user specifications of the information system, or changes to it, so that they can easily be realised and tested. The primary result of this process is the functional or logic design, a non-technical description of its intended operation.

Issues
Development of the process stages
There are many options for developing the design process. The development method is selected by quality management depending on the system, environment and organisation. The following issues are relevant:
- general design approach (waterfall, incremental, prototyping);
- division into stages (overall, details);
- approaches (functional, technical);
- methodologies and diagrams;
- representation of data, functions and time aspects (sequence) in the design.

These choices may be made for each project or system, or for the organisation as a whole. ASL does not cover the development methods (see also section 3.2.1).

Design development
The specifications of an application or change are complete once the data, functions (queries and operations applied to the data) and time aspects (relationships and sequence of the functions) have been described. Time aspects are often not specifically referred to in the documentation.

Differences between development and enhancement
The methods and the detailing of the issues are similar to those in system development. This is to be expected as the systems were previously developed (and then transferred to maintenance and enhancement) and because enhancement often includes significant changes to or even complete replacement of large part of applications.

However, in practice a slightly different approach is required. Application management includes a number of rigid frameworks: the system exists, and the changes will have to be compatible with the design choices made for the system. There is less freedom in the design, the deadlines are often more rigid, and we know that anything which cannot be resolved now will have to be dealt with later. In other words, the requirements are stricter and the options are more limited. These options affect enhancement whenever there is a choice to be made, and they often necessitate compromises. It is rarely possible to provide the perfect solution. Consequently the process often includes a step in which a choice is made between the potential solutions.

Specification types
There are several methods to develop clear specifications. Sometimes a short description is enough, functional designs are also used frequently, and sometimes technical solutions are used (prototyping). The result of the process design is an unambiguous, clearly defined specification of the users' requirements which is usually referred to as the user specification.

Activities
The design activities are normally specified by the selected development method and methodology. Most development methods include the following steps:

Detailing the requirements:
- thorough analysis of the requirements or specified change;
- translation of the information to information needs and information requirements or changes in the information requirements;
- outlining relevant parts of the system.

Identifying solution(s):
- identify the potential options for solutions;
- identify advantages and disadvantages, consider these in the context of the constraints;
- select a solution.

Detail the solution:
- determine and detail the specifications;
- draw up functional test specifications;
- document the design and any changes to it.

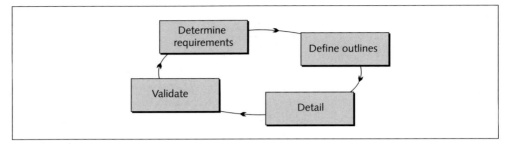

Figure 21 Development process stages

Validation:
- internal quality assurance;
- feedback to customer;
- approval by customer.

Management:
- monitor progress;
- evaluate progress, results and the process.

Results
Design documentation:
- system documentation (definition of the detailed and approved specifications): description of the functions of the changed application, data model and process flow;
- any changes to the specifications;
- test specifications and test design: description of the test methods and test cases to be used.

Progress data (planning and control, etc.):
- planning and progress;
- evaluations and any problems.

Relationships
Impact analysis
Design is a routine step in the enhancement and renovation process. The process logically follows after the impact analysis. The impact analysis report provides input for the design process.

Functional management
Functional management provides the information for the functional specification of the change. Functional management approves the defined specifications. The functional design is often used as the basic definition.

Chapter 5 Enhancement and renovation

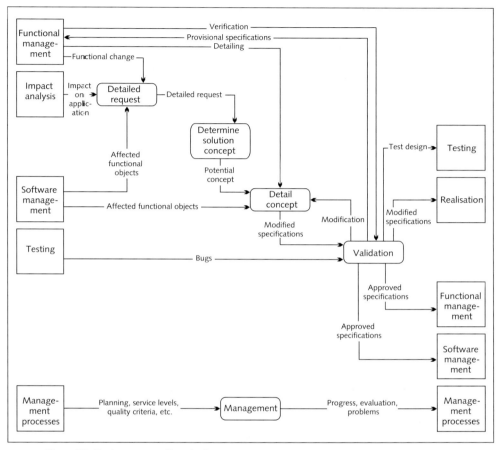

Figure 22 Design process flowchart

Realisation
The design (the result of the design process) provides the input for the realisation (program development) process. The changes defined in the designs and specifications are created in this process.

Testing
The test specifications provide input to the test process. Tests may reveal bugs, questions or incomplete elements which have to be resolved in the design.

Management processes
The process is controlled by the management processes. The expected effort and cycle time are indicated by planning and control. The actual program development (progress report) is reported to this process.

The quality criteria and methods (quality system) provide input from quality management. They are not included in the flow chart as they are common to all processes. Service level management contributes agreements and service levels. The program development, evaluations, problems, etc. are then reported to these processes.

Software control and distribution
Documentation logistics is included under software control and distribution. Designs are made available and approved designs have to be stored and logged by software control and distribution.

5.4 Realisation

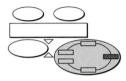

Objectives
Realisation (program development) aims to convert the specifications from the design process into definite and correct changes to the automated information system.

Issues
Division into stages
The process stages are based on the same structure used in most processes in this enhancement cluster. Firstly, the requirement is clearly defined, e.g. using the functional design or a prototype. This is then used to define the outlines: the way in way the change will be implemented, the technical design. This design is then developed in detail after which the changes are realised and tested.

To make specific and correct changes to the automated information system we have to translate the logical specifications into a technical solution. This is normally done in a technical design stage.

Design and documentation
A technical design is a description of the technical structure of the information system or the change to be made. It amounts to a translation of the functional demand into the selected technical solution. This is not always specifically included in the system documentation. In some cases the technical structure and development are integrated with the functional design. The disadvantage of this is that the discussions with the functional manager may address inappropriate issues, i.e. technical choices.

The change is realised by writing or modifying programs. The structure and selected solution used within a program may be complex. In that event additional software documentation will be required. This may be provided by including appropriate comments in the programs. Another option is to develop or update a program description or specifically including the information in the detailed technical design. The selected option is specified by the quality system.

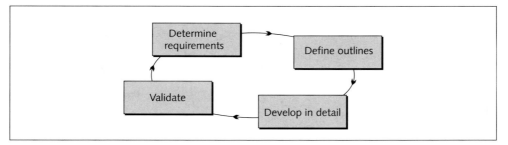

Figure 23 Steps in the realisation process

Relationship with software control
The first step in the realisation process is to use the detailed design to review the affected programs, which may be different from the change set defined earlier. Programs may not be affected by the change if their structure is appropriate. However, more programs will sometimes have to be modified. This is undesirable as it will require another review to determine if these programs or objects have been changed in the intervening period by another release or corrective maintenance.

The result of the realisation step is the change package: the set of programs or data items which will indeed change. After the successful completion of the tests, software control and distribution will have to transfer these changed or new programs to the production environment. More information about change packages and change sets is included in section 6.2 (Software control and distribution).

Relationship with operations
The realisation process amounts to a translation of the functional requirement and the technical solution. The technical solution operates within technical management. Consequently, technical management often needs information, for example about the files used by the programs, the requirements to run the programs and systems, and the dependencies between operational elements. This information, the operating documentation, can be defined in an operating file or production file. The way in which this information is communicated and defined has to be agreed with the technical management organisation.

Activities
Plan and determine the technical impact:
- validate the starting point;
- identify affected elements in detail.

Design the technical solution:
- determine the solution in outlines;
- determine the division into relevant changes;

- determine the approach;
- discuss/assess the approach;
- define technical test specifications;
- document the technical solution.

Realise the plan:
- modify software;
- modify data objects;
- modify any supplementary objects (e.g. operations information);
- document the software.

Test the software:
- test the software to identify programming errors (white box test);
- test the change: all modified programs and files.

Management:
- realisation planning;
- progress reporting;
- evaluation.

Results

New or modified documentation:
- technical designs: description of the selected technical solution and approach (ideally with supporting arguments);
- software documentation: description of the operation of the program;
- technical test specifications (test design);
- product documentation: information for technical management (how the system operates, and relevant conditions).

New or modified system:
- new or changed software (provisional change packages);
- new or changed data definitions (including any conversions required).

Test results:
- unit test results;
- any test data or scripts.

Management information:
- progress reports;
- evaluation of the process and results.

Chapter 5 Enhancement and renovation

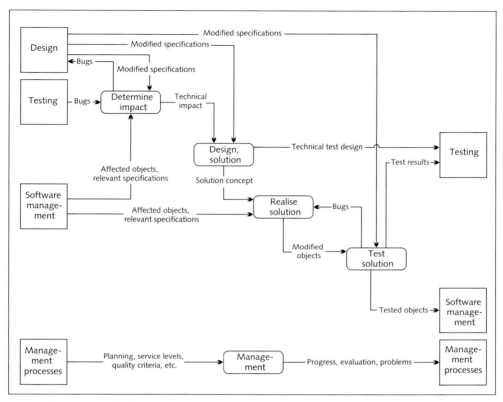

Figure 24 Realisation flowchart

Relationships
Design
The primary input for the realisation process is provided by the specifications provided by the design process. These were defined as specifications or designs (which may have been modified) and may be distributed by software control.

Testing
The correctness of the modified or new application is verified by the testing process. This process may reveal bugs or shortcomings which have to be remedied in the realisation process.

Software control and distribution
The software and technical documentation are provided by software control. The changed programs are documentation are also filed by software control and distribution which then distributes them to the appropriate environments.

Management processes
The plans and schedules, expected cycle time and realisation effort should have been identified in the planning and control process. The progress reports with information about the progress and use of allocated resources also go to this process which will change the plans if required. Where relevant, the service level management process provides service levels as input. The completeness and correctness of the realisation (i.e. do we provide what we agreed?) are reported to service level management and quality management. The quality during this stage is monitored by quality management using audits, random checks, quality assurance and peer reviews. The quality system under which the application is implemented is the responsibility of quality management.

5.5 Testing

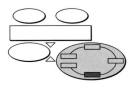

Objectives
Testing includes the activities to determine if what we have designed has indeed been implemented. Testing also ensures that the implemented application can be maintained and operated. The objective of the testing process is to ensure that the required changes have been implemented in accordance with the specification and that the changed application will behave correctly.

Issues
Testing is essential to prevent inoperative or faulty systems entering service. Many methods and tools have been developed to structure testing. These methodologies (e.g. Tmap) are not covered by ASL.

Ideally, testing will be considered from the start. This is incorporated in ASL in aspects of the design and realisation processes. The design process includes test design (i.e. what is to be tested, and how?). This is where the design of the test cases (test data and test scripts) starts. It is often useful to archive the test cases and to modify or extend then for a new release. The tests are carried out in reverse order of the change process: the implemented programs are tested first, then the combination, and then the combination in its environment.

Unit test
Used to verify if the realised or changed programs meet the relevant requirements. This activity is part of realisation, it is used immediately to verify if the product made in this step complies with the specifications.

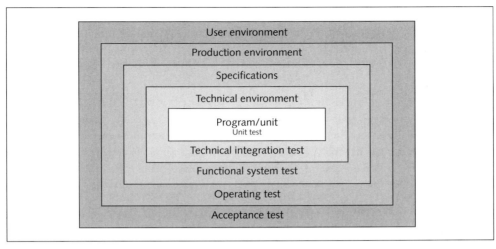

Figure 25 Tests

Technical system test
This test verifies if:
- what is implemented complies with the relevant specifications;
- the changed elements work as part of the whole (i.e. the test is not limited to the changed element);
- the whole still allows enhancement and meets the quality criteria agreed further to maintenance and enhancement issues.

Functional system test
This test verifies if the:
- changes were made correctly;
- information system as a whole provides the agreed functionality;
- system still works in functional terms;
- functional documents comply with the agreed quality criteria.

Production test
This test is often carried out by the operational organisation or technical management to determine if the:
- changed or renovated system, when operating, meets the primary requirements (e.g. cycle time, transaction time, etc.) which are often specified by service level management;
- system meets the secondary requirements (e.g. production documentation, opportunities for review, etc.).

Acceptance test
The customer or functional management use this test to verify if the:
- agreed elements have been implemented (for sign-off);
- system can indeed be used by the user organisation. In this case, the customer organisation also tests its own quality.

The first test stage (unit test), forms part of the realisation process, it provides a check internal to the process. The last stage, the acceptance test, is not included in application management but in functional management. The acceptance test is undertaken during the implementation. However, the follow-up of the outcome of an acceptance test follows the routine test arrangements.

Activities
Technical system test:
- prepare the tests (create test cases or update test sets);
- undertake the tests;
- determine the impact of bugs;
- evaluate and determine potential solutions;
- have the bugs fixed.

Functional (logical) system test:
- prepare the tests;
- undertake the tests;
- determine the impact of bugs;
- evaluate and determine potential solutions;
- have the bugs fixed.

Support production test:
- support the tests;
- determine the impact of bugs;
- evaluate and determine potential solutions;
- have the bugs fixed.

Management:
- make progress reports;
- make bug reports;
- evaluate the process and results.

Chapter 5 Enhancement and renovation

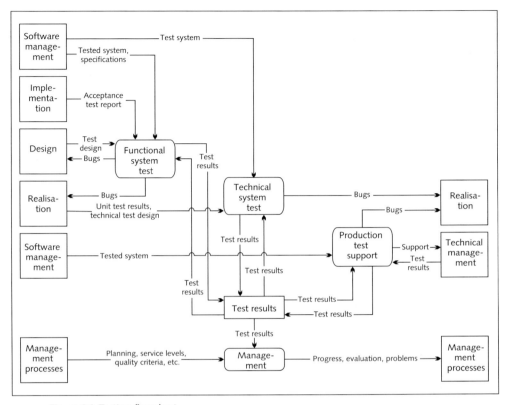

Figure 26 Testing flowchart

Results

Test products:
- test results (expected and actual results);
- test reports (number of bugs, status, responsibilities for follow-up);
- bugs/questions.

Management progress:
- progress reports;
- evaluation.

Test support:
- test cases/test sets;
- test software/scripts.

Relationships

Design and realisation
The tests will reveal bugs and questions. These have to be answered or solved by the realisation (implementation) and design processes. The design process provides the functional test design. The realisation process routes the results of the acceptance tests to the test process.

Implementation
The implementation process routes the results of the acceptance tests to the test process.

Software control and distribution
The versions of the system to be tested are provided by software control and distribution. The test sets and test cases and any special software for the tests may be archived and reused if software control and distribution archives them. Software control and distribution issues the appropriate versions of the application objects to be tested to the relevant environments such as the system test environment, functional system test, acceptance test, etc.

Management processes
Planning and progress are discussed with planning and control. Evaluations and any problems are routed to quality management. The testing system (including the test strategy, test techniques, quality attributes as described in the test plans, etc.) forms part of the quality system. Results of the acceptance test and any impact on service levels and agreements with customers are routed to service level management.

5.6 Implementation

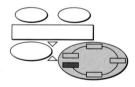

Objectives
The implementation process includes all activities to be carried out to make the proposals for change (from change management) effective in operations and data processing. The objective of the implementation is to define the conditions for the perfect operation of the new version of the application and to complete the enhancement process.

Issues
Completing a change requires activities in three areas:
- supporting the user organisation when it starts using the change;
- supporting the technical manager when it is introduced into the production environment;
- completing the change and protecting the application objects.

Finally, the implementation process also undertakes activities to complete the assignment.

The acceptance test is the last stage, it is used by the functional manager to verify all changes have been introduced correctly, from the user's perspective, and provides the basis for the sign-off.

Activities
Preparing for operations:
- support the preparation of processing and installation;
- support or implement changes to data definitions in the production environment, support technical conversions;
- prepare and support the scheduling of data processing operations (see also availability management);
- preparing the instructions for transferring the change to the operational environment.

Preparing the user organisation:
- support the preparation of the acceptance test;
- support the acceptance test (data, queries, processing of the test results);
- support functional management for the introduction in the user organisation, e.g. support changes to user manuals, support functional conversions (functional control parameters).

Preparing the completion of the release:
- archive documents, prepare the sign-off, start evaluations;
- fix bugs further to the acceptance test.

Completion of the assignment:
- assignment sign-off;
- production order;
- status report to change management.

Management:
- progress reports;
- evaluation.

Results
Supporting commissioning:
- support acceptance test;
- any information from the acceptance test;
- support introduction in the user organisation.

Supporting introduction into production:
- supplementary production information;
- potential changes to production schedules;
- support for changes to data definitions and conversions.

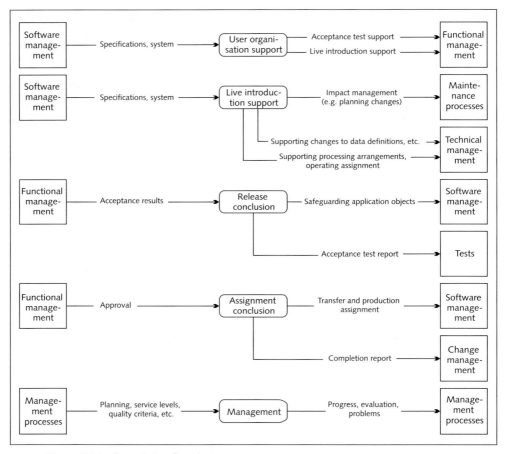

Figure 27 Implementation flowchart

Relationships
Functional management
The implementation process provides functional management with support for undertaking the acceptance test and introduction into the user organisation (supporting user manuals, changes to functional control parameters, etc.). Functional management provides the implementation process with the release sign-off, change, and renovation assignment.

Technical management
The implementation process provides support and information to technical management so that the release can be introduced into the production operations. Examples include supporting changes to data definitions, providing information about files, operations and steps, order of the operations, supporting the development of installation procedures, etc. The instructions to technical management for introducing the change into the production operations are also routed through the implementation process.

Maintenance processes
The experiences from the production test and acceptance test (e.g. concerning required computer capacity, availability and continuity) are routed to the maintenance processes. For example, the release may require new schedules or changes to the production schedules. These are communicated to availability management.

Software control and distribution
The implementation process informs software control and distribution that the release is complete and that the products in the change package can be transferred to the production environment(s) at the specified time.

Change management
The changes in the status of the release (approved, used in production) are communicated to change management.

Testing
The results of the acceptance test are communicated to the testing process.

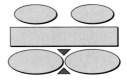

CHAPTER 6

Connecting processes

The ASL messages
— The connecting processes synchronise the maintenance processes and the enhancement processes. They provide the logistics of application management.
— These processes are essential to professional application management. However, in practice they are often underdeveloped.

6.1 Introduction

The connecting processes provide the synchronisation and coordination between the two operational process clusters.

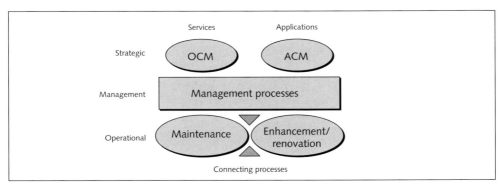

Figure 28 The ASL model

The processes change management and software control and distribution provide the connections between the two cycles: the maintenance cycle and the enhancement/renovation cycle. Change management provides the channel towards enhancement, and software control provides towards maintenance. Change management provides the logistics of the changes, while software control looks after the information system objects. Both processes also support the enhancement processes.

77

6.2 Change management

Objectives
Change management provides a means to identify, prioritise, initiate, evaluate and adjust the changes which have to be made to the application. The objective of change management is to ensure that a standardised method is used to implement changes to applications, so that changes are coordinated and prioritised, in order to change the functionality of the application.

The change management process collates and clusters all changes, and schedules them for releases or projects. This process is undertaken in consultation with the customer and validated by impact analysis. It results in the definition of the final change and agreements about the further development, cost and delivery date of the release. The implementation requires an effective project definition and preparation: defining the project, process and product requirements, planning, budget and project structure. In essence, change management provides a channel towards enhancement.

Issues
Changes are desirable or essential changes to the application objects. These include programs and files, as well as documentation and other objects. A release is a set of combined changes which are introduced together, at the same time.

Reasons for changes
Changes have a variety of reasons: incidents, requests for change from functional management (legislative changes, new products, new reports, removal of functions), quality management (in the event of problems or measures to improve quality), service level management (changes to realise agreements made earlier).

Change status
There are at least three change statuses: changes which have been received but not yet followed-up or scheduled (desirable, request for change), changes which are included in enhancement (in progress), and changes which have been completed (signed-off).

Change implementation
Changes may be so extensive that they are divided over a number of releases. Depending on the way the organisation wants to arrange this, the change can be divided into a number of changes to be included in each release, or subchanges can be used. In application management it is not unusual to find that changes are only implemented after a long time; this is often quite different from technical management. The reason for the difference is that some changes are quite clearly less important than others (production interruptions, legislative changes, etc.) which means that less important changes may keep

Chapter 6 Connecting processes

the status 'desirable' for a long period. Consequently, the average time required to complete a change is not always an effective performance indicator.

Activities
Logging (managing) changes:
- receive and list requests for change;
- file and log requests for change and the associated initial details (scope, cycle time, priority, origin).

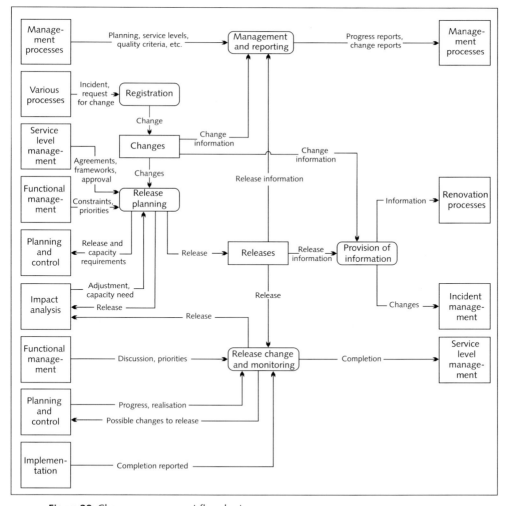

Figure 29 Change management flowchart

Preparation and scheduling of releases:
- list premises and conditions for releases;
- allocate and cluster requests for change to releases;
- determine if the releases comply with the premises and conditions;
- prepare decisions on the release;
- initiate the change round/release.

Updating and monitoring releases:
- where necessary, update the release based on further information from the impact analysis or later stages of the enhancement/renovation process;
- monitor interaction between releases;
- monitor completion, and that requests for change are deleted after the completion of a change.

Management and reporting:
- report on changes to be considered, outstanding, completed, etc., and the scale of the backlog;
- write evaluations and reports about problems, time, financial aspects, etc.

Results

Change records (changes):
- changes and their status;
- initial indications of their scale and impact;
- priorities.

Release records (releases):
- release;
- underlying changes;
- starting time, cycle time, scale;
- status.

Information about changes and releases:
- changes in a release;
- completion of the release and its changes.

Management information:
- change reports: reports on changes to be considered, outstanding, completed, etc., and the scale of the backlog;
- problems, evaluations, progress, capacity.

Relationships
Operational processes
Incident management is one of the primary sources of changes. Incident management contributes incidents and faults, and functional management provides specifications and assignments (sometimes via incident management).

The details of a release are subject to impact analysis and other processes. Impact analysis determines the budget and impact of a release. This may lead to modifications to a release which are then realised by the other enhancement processes. Information about the progress and status of a release are then reported by these processes. Implementation provides information about the completion of the release.

Management processes
Required changes may originate in problems and suggested improvements. Often communication about this type of change is provided by quality management, sometimes via incident management.

The estimates about the releases and modifications to them are reported to the planning and control process which may revise them on the basis of risk factors, available capacity, etc. The progress of the release is monitored by planning and control. Any modifications which are required to the delivery date, etc. of the release are communicated by planning and control. Modification of the details of the release is the responsibility of change management.

The planning of the release (changes, dates and possible the scope of the effort) and the status of the release are communicated to service level management, as these agreements are essentially service levels.

Software control and distribution
There is close interaction with this process, in essence software control and distribution (if it is set up properly) is the technical equivalent of change management. The progress of a release to the next stage is also apparent within software control and distribution. The term 'release' is an essential concept in software control and distribution. These information flows are not illustrated to prevent confusion.

6.3 Software control and distribution

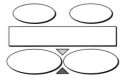

Objectives
Software control and distribution includes the processes associated with the maintenance and distribution of operational application objects (program objects and supporting objects such as documentation, data definitions, etc.). Software control and distribution aims to provide the right application objects (or information about them), to the right processes, at the right time.

This process has to provide secure procedures to limit the risks of unauthorised access, change or deletion. The process can be considered as a product channel: modified application components are transferred to operations (technical management), and information about them is provided to the maintenance processes. This process is also responsible for the logistics affecting objects between the stages of the enhancement process.

Issues
The process within enhancement. The software control and distribution process can be fairly complex. For example, an application may have several overlapping versions and releases.

The impact analysis and any additional work is used to identify and document the change set. The change set is the set of objects which may be modified further to a release. In effect, they are the objects which are allocated to a release or change.

The enhancement processes result in the change package. The change package is the set of objects which have been changed and approved and which will be transferred to the production environment (in the wider sense, it also includes the system documentation environment).

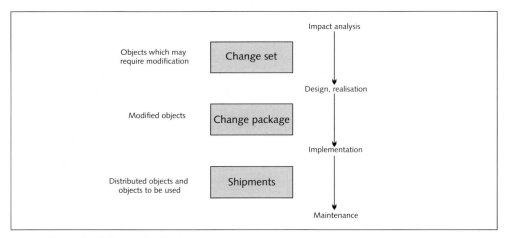

Figure 30 Software distribution

In reality there may be several change packages in which case there will also be several releases of an application.
The distribution to the production environment can be divided into stages. In this case several distributions (shipments) will be necessary or desirable. A shipment is a set of

changed objects which together have to be transferred to one or more production environments, and accompanied by the implementation instructions. Several releases may be in preparation concurrently. It is therefore possible that objects are changed in another release, but not yet transferred to the production environment. Change sets and change packages can be used to identify overlaps between releases. Any such interference requires additional consideration: the changes being made to the objects will have to be synchronised in the logistics process.

> **Example: implementing a patch**
> A program is modified because of a problem. A quick fix is made and introduced into production. The program is also updated as part of a release. Because the overlap was neglected there was no synchronisation and the old problem recurs after introducing the release.

More than one version
Different versions of applications (information systems) may be used at different locations (operating environments) and possibly even by different operating organisations. This is quite a common occurrence with packages and distributed environments. This means that configuration management has to know which version is used in each environment. Consequently, there is no one-to-one relationship between the CMDBs of technical management and application management.

Different software versions or releases may be running at different locations. The CMDB used for configuration management by application management may therefore contain details of several software releases. Hence, there is a many-to-many relationship between software control and the CMDB used by application management.

More than one version in technical management
Several releases of an application may also be stored by technical management. This is often undesirable as it requires additional effort by the technical management environment.

Activities
Logging objects covered by the enhancement process:
- recording the change set: flagging that objects may be changed by a release;
- where necessary transferring objects between the environments in the enhancement process;
- transferring objects to production environments.

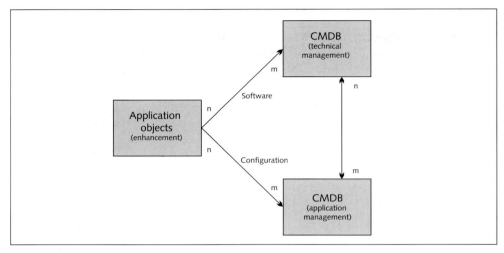

Figure 31 Configurations

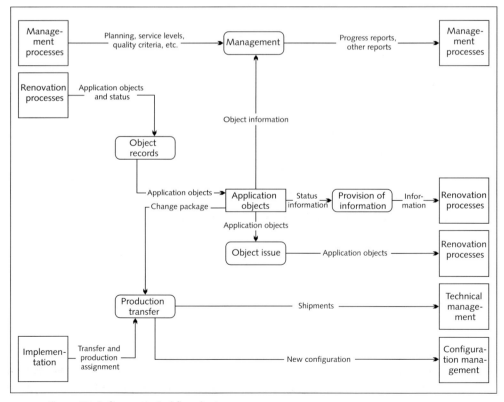

Figure 32 Software control flowchart

Issuing objects:
- archiving versions of objects;
- issuing various types of documentation to design or realisation;
- issuing software items (programs, etc.) to realisation, testing, acceptance testing, etc.

Providing information to the enhancement process:
- identifying related objects (further to a change) and defining change sets;
- identifying potential interference between change sets;
- issuing software and documentation in a specified status of a specified release;
- defining the change package.

Transferring to the production environment;
- determining the potential shipments, on the basis of the available change packages;
- approving transfer to production;
- transferring shipments to the production environment (in the broader sense);
- communicating updated information about the new or changed application objects to configuration management.

Results
Application object deliveries:
- change packages;
- change sets;
- shipments.

Supporting transfers between environments and stages:
- transfer software and documentation;
- transfer to production;
- information about the new configuration.

Status and object information:
- support identification of the impact and relationships;
- interference between releases;
- other information.

Management:
- reports;
- evaluations, problems.

Relationships
The software control and distribution process has particularly close relationships with change management and configuration management. It also supports the various enhancement processes which also creates a number of relationships.

Change management
Change management provides essential information to software control and distribution. Each release is included in the change management system. A release is often the basic unit used by software control and distribution, and used to issue objects. It is also most important that the information about the progress from change management and software control is correct (e.g. whether a release is in the realisation stage or the test stage).

Configuration management
Information about current and potential new application objects is communicated to configuration management. Ideally, configuration management and software control together will always make it possible to identify what software is used where, and how it was created.

Renovation processes
In the renovation processes, software control is responsible for the logistics of existing objects, objects to be changed and changed objects. If the organisation functions effectively, the products of the renovation processes always return to software control. The application objects, changes, and status changes are received and communicated to the renovation processes. Software control also looks after several environments, such as the acceptance environment. An impact analysis normally depends on software control and distribution to determine the relationships within the system, and to identify which objects may have been changed, and where.

Implementation
Acceptance by functional management confirms that the renovation processes have been completed. Further to this the object may be transferred to production.

Management processes
The structure and operation of the software control system is covered by quality management. Change management informs service level management about the progress and completion of a release. Software control and distribution provides change management with evidence about the progress. There is also routine management information such as problems, evaluations, use of resources and progress, number of objects, etc.

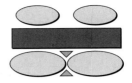

CHAPTER 7

Management processes

The ASL messages
— The primary management issues are time, money, external quality (service levels) and internal quality.
— The management processes are forecasting (predictive), current (monitoring and adjustment), and historical (evaluation).
— There is a learning curve before an organisation will be able to account for the results of using ASL. Professional organisations are expected to be accountable.
— Management processes do not only operate top-down but also bottom-up to ensure that the policies are put into practice. In other words, the management processes not only send information to the strategic processes, but also receive information from them.
— Management processes focus on hard information.

7.1 Introduction

The management processes are at the centre of the ASL framework and are described in this chapter. We will start by providing a framework for these processes.

In the ASL framework, the management processes occupy a position between the strategic processes and the operational processes. Management is normally applied at several levels within an organisation. This means that a number of issues have to be considered when setting up and implementing these processes:
- management always operates at several levels;
- special consideration should be given to the interaction between strategy and operations: ASL does not assume a pure top-down management style.

These elements are discussed in following sections.

Management issues

The management processes are concerned with four issues:
- time: delivery time, required capacity and effort, realisation of the whole;
- money: funds available for the provision of services as a whole;
- the quality of the services provided and the way it is monitored;
- the expectations of customers and suppliers and the agreements made with them (service levels).

These four issues are reflected in the four processes in this cluster:
- planning and control covers the realisation of the plans and the control of resources, time, money, human resources;
- cost management covers financial aspects;
- quality management covers the internal quality, the quality of the organisation, product, work and resources;
- service level management covers the management of external quality and agreements with the customer.

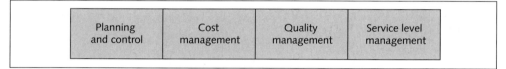

Figure 33 Management processes

There may be conflicts between these issues, and balancing the relevant interests is an essential element of managing application management processes. Planning and control is the umbrella process as it manages the realisation and deployment of resources.

These four processes are similar to elements of the EFQM model. For example, the quality management issues have a major impact on the "People results".[2] "Customer results" are largely dependent on the extent to which the agreed service levels are met (which is the responsibility of service level management). Shareholder satisfaction is closely dependent on the cost management process.

Of course, the issues have many interactions and dependencies. The planning and control process manages these dependencies, and provides a central focus for the other management processes.

---

[2] Of course, this is also affected by issues outside the quality management process. This also applies to issues outside the quality management process.

Management aspects
The management processes occupy a position between the operational processes and the strategic processes. Within ASL the management processes are broad as the approach is one of integrated planning and management. The integration has two aspects:
- the management processes take both strategic and operational approaches;
- the management processes consider the past, present and future and therefore provide evaluation, management and planning.

Integrated: management as well as operations
The integrated approach means that the interests and preferences of all processes and process clusters in ASL provide input to the management processes and that they should be balanced. Thus, the management processes must consider both strategic and operational issues – the management view is top-down as well as bottom-up. Strategy should be reflected in activities or changes to the operating processes (including the capacity to implement the change), and operational experience must provide input to strategic considerations.

In this way, the strategy will be accepted on the shop floor and maintenance and enhancement experience flows back to the higher management levels. This ensures that the strategies tie in with reality.

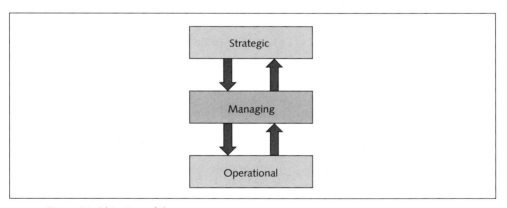

Figure 34 Objectives of the management processes

Learning and optimising
The processes consider the past, present and future. Firm agreements and service levels are an essential element of ASL. A professional application management organisation is accountable for its results. This can only be achieved by looking forward and identifying any risks which might interfere with the objectives. Monitoring the present, i.e. assessing how things are going and making adjustments, is also essential. Lastly, we have to look

back on the results and evaluate them. To what extent did we do what we wanted to accomplish, what are the lessons learned, and what do we do with them? Identifying the root causes of any problems is also essential.

Levels of management
Application management usually has a structure with several levels of management. Examples of such levels include:
- release (enhancement round);
- department;
- the organisation as a whole.

Within ASL, the structure of the management processes is the same on each level, but the areas covered are different and therefore the emphasis may also be different. In terms of efficiency and effectiveness it is advisable to link the management processes at the different levels where possible. Some examples:
- Higher levels may serve as an escalation level, as a level to solve problems, as a safety net. Planning and control is an example: if it is concluded that the release has a backlog additional capacity may be deployed by a higher level.
- The departmental quality system can be used as a blueprint which is customised into quality systems for each project.
- Strategy is developed into actions at the lower levels. The strategic policy of the application management organisation to adopt a new tool is implemented by using the tool for a release and making the required investment, e.g. in additional capacity.
- The reverse is also possible. Persistent problems affecting a number of releases or projects are considered in a broader perspective at a higher level, and permanently solved. Version problems affecting a number of projects can result in the introduction of a version management system throughout the organisation.

7.2 Planning and control

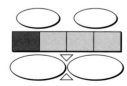

Objective
The objective of planning and control is to ensure that the agreed services are provided at the right time and with the right capacity, by deploying the right IT and human resources at the right time. Planning and control can be considered as time and capacity management in the broader sense. The time at which the agreed services are to be delivered is agreed with the customer. This concerns both project activities (within enhancement and renovation) and continuous activities (maintenance). Managing both these aspects, often by the same department and people, is the main challenge of application management.

Planning and control is the central and major management process as in the end, everything has to be realised through the human resources.

As with the other management processes, this process normally operates at several levels, such as planning and monitoring releases, the project, the department and the organisation.

Issues
Available capacity
The planning and control process is not limited to scheduling operational activities such as maintenance and enhancement. The use of resources in the following areas should also be considered:
- Contribution to strategic processes. Obviously, strategic processes interface with operations which means that relevant personnel have to contribute to these processes.
- The demands and investments related to choices made in the strategic processes (possibly received from functional management or the business management processes). Examples include improving the technical quality of the application by restructuring a calculation program, migrating to the new release of the development environment, etc.
- The management processes. Reserving capacity for quality management, cost management or service level management.
- Required improvements associated with the management processes, for example improving financial reporting in the organisation and improving the quality organisation.

Other objectives are also relevant, such as meeting return on investment or cost reduction objectives.

Budgeting
Drawing up the enhancement budget is an important element of the planning and control process. The actual budgets are mostly drawn up in the other processes. A change round is often budgeted during the impact analysis. Appropriate methods include enhancement function point systems, Product Breakdown Structure and Work Breakdown Structure.

We have to go beyond these activities as the real world is more complex. There are many reasons to view the outcomes in a broader perspective, such as risks associated with the current quality of the application, service levels to be provided, available experience and expertise, need for a flawless introduction, experience from other projects, holidays, etc. These adjustments are made within planning and control and require additional sources of information and tools. These include a range of indicators such as productivity factors, availability rates, risk analyses, etc. This information is often provided by other processes.

Activities

Planning:
- planning objectives, etc.;
- developing objectives into activities;
- identifying risks and appropriate measures;
- assessing the available and required capacity;
- capacity scheduling;
- updating and monitoring indicators (function parameters, enhancement function points, availability and chargeable hours indicators, etc.).

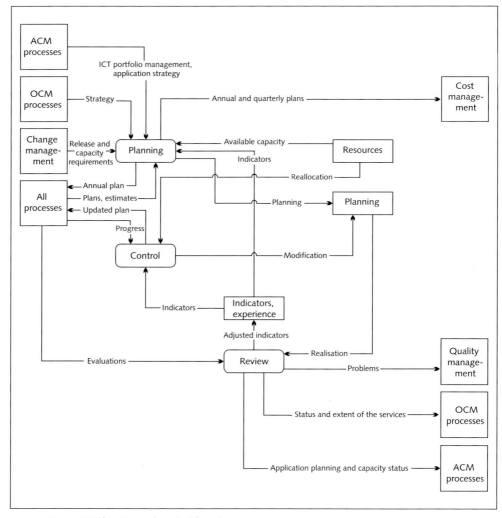

Figure 35 Planning and control flowchart

Control:
- monitoring the working hours available (illness, holidays, training, etc.);
- monitoring the hours spent on assignments;
- progress monitoring;
- updating further to the current situation;
- rearranging tasks, reallocations, adjusting milestones, reducing the scope of the assignment.

Review:
- evaluating the results, possibly on the basis of unit rates;
- learning from and filing the lessons learned;
- recognising problems and making proposals for improvement.

Results

Control plans:
- annual plan: planned projects and continuing activities for the year ahead, time schedules/division into stages/releases, capacity and human resources to be deployed;
- quarterly plan: planning and actual performance during the past quarter, planning the period ahead;
- project plan/release plan: objectives/changes to be implemented, organisational structure, capacity, milestones, timelines.

Resources:
- available capacity and expertise.

Planning:
- schedules (detailed plans);
- allocation of resources to assignments;
- allocation reports;
- budgets.

Indicators, experiences:
- process indicators, risk factors and supplements, additional overhead rates, function point factors.

Reports:
- project reports and progress reports.

Relationships
The planning and control process occupies a central position in the model. Even more so than the other management processes it has relationships with all the operational processes. It is responsible for the deployment, planning and progress monitoring of these processes. It also has links with strategic processes. A large proportion of the activities and investments of application management relate to the enhancement and renovation processes. The capacity required for these can vary greatly and is largely dependent on the changes to be made to the application. Within the renovation processes there are two processes which provide the input to analyse and manage this: change management and impact analysis.

Change management
Change management defines the constraints and content of a release and thereby defines the work package to be realised which has to be scheduled by planning and control.

Impact analysis
Impact analysis provides estimates of the expenditure and scheduling of releases and changes, possibly through change management.

Operational processes
Planning and control also monitors planning and progress in all other processes. These processes submit estimates to planning and control. The capacity and planning are allocated to these processes, for example through the annual plan. These processes report to planning and control on progress and the use of resources.

Other management processes
Quality management and service level management can make proposals (requests for investment) to realise changes or new objectives. These processes also report on progress and the use of resources. Planning and control provides the primary input for the cost management process. Cost management information is largely provided by planning and control (hours, use of allocated resources). Cost management uses this information to set targets and raise invoices.

OCM processes
The planning and control process provides information to the OCM processes, such as the available service volume, available capacity and experience with it, and trends in these areas. This information is particularly valuable for skills definition and account definition. In essence, the planning and control process also monitors the realisation of the objectives and strategy described in the service delivery definition. Planning and control allocates resources and monitors progress.

ACM processes
Information about the capacity deployed for applications and productivity standards for application enhancement provide status information for the life cycle management and ICT portfolio management processes.

7.3 Cost management

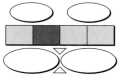

Objective
Cost management includes the processes to control and charge for the costs of providing IT services. Cost management provides financial management data to strike the best possible balance between cost and performance. Effective cost management, based on an integrated approach will clearly identify the financial impact of the available choices. The best choice is then selected in consultation with the customer. The objective of cost management is to ensure that the costs of applications and application management are transparent and cost-effective, that adequate financial data is provided to support investment decisions, and that financial agreements are concluded with the customer to ensure the cost-effective use of applications and application management.

Issues
In the context of this process it is useful to distinguish between internal and external service providers as this determines the emphasis of the services. If an external service provider is used there will be a finance department looking after the accounts, rates and invoicing. In this case the ICT organisation will also have clear revenues, which are essential to the survival of the service provider. The communications with the finance department will usually follow the pattern shown in the figure.

Internal application management departments do not usually invoice for their services. However, invoicing would make both the customer and the application management organisation more aware of the costs. This reflects the growing trend to make internal application management organisations and users more professional and more cost-aware. Financial record-keeping is not included in application management.

We have to know what the costs are, and how they are charged. ASL promotes firm agreements for greater professionalism, transparency and control. These agreements are concluded before the services are provided, and the costs are charged irrespective of the actual performance, as long as the assignment is carried out within the agreed constraints.

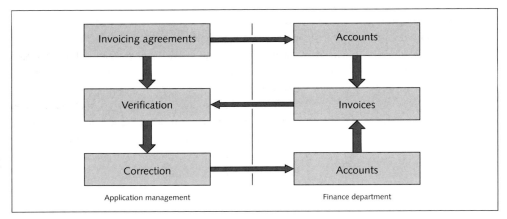

Figure 36 Relationship between the finance department and application management

> **Example:**
> A fixed price is charged for introducing a release. Fixed prices are the opposite of reimbursable charging where the actual costs are calculated and charged.

Unit costs are charged to the customer or user, or used to give an indication of the costs (see also Figure 3). These may be directly related to the costs (hours spent on the project), or expressed in terms or units which are clearer or under the customer's control (e.g. financial transactions or salary statements). The latter case is another example of firm agreements. Thus, the invoicing units are not always directly related to the cost price.

Even if there are no firm agreements, we have to know the cost price, although this is often difficult to determine. Cost prices reflect the actual cost of service units and include all indirect costs.

> **Example: design hour**
> The cost price includes not only the designer's salary, but also other costs such as social security, workstation, building, secretarial support, overheads and training. As these costs are difficult to determine this should be left to the finance department. There are many costs at higher levels which have to be included in the rate.

Activities
Budgeting:
- including the expected costs and allocation to subbudgets;

- monitoring budget expenditure during the year and updating the budgets (quarterly reports, etc.);
- identifying and updating indicators (when using firm agreements and unit rates).

Budget monitoring:
- monitoring budgeted costs and revenues;
- communicating budget agreements and verifying invoices;
- correcting invoices or cost reports;
- identifying risks and taking appropriate measures.

Budget review:
- evaluating the financial performance;
- identifying the lessons learned;
- updating indicators;
- identifying problems and appropriate improvements.

Results
The results depend on the management level at which they are reviewed. They may relate to the financial return of an assignment or project, or those of a department or business unit.

Invoicing information:
- unit rates and quantities;
- corrected unit rates and quantities.

Financial expertise:
- indicators;
- invoicing and charging models.

Financial plans:
- annual financial plan, budget;
- quarterly budgets;
- monthly budgets.

Budget expenditure:
- budget and actual figures;
- cost and revenue trends.

Relationships
ACM processes (Application Cycle Management). Cost management provides information to the ACM processes (life cycle management and ICT portfolio management) about the cost of applications and services, and any changes in the costs. These processes may

ASL A Framework for Application Management

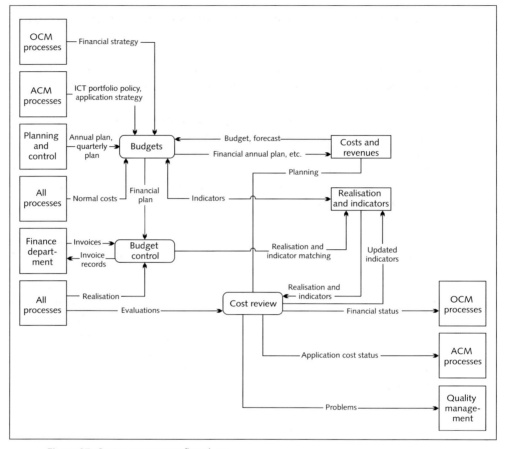

Figure 37 Cost management flowchart

suggest infrastructure investments or hiring external expertise or human resources (in renovation plans or ICT portfolio management).

OCM processes (Organisation Cycle Management). The OCM processes provide strategic outlines for the costs of application management and any investments with a financial impact on the organisation.

Management processes. Planning and control provides information about the deployed capacity (hours), assignments to be arranged and assignment progress further to the deployed capacity. Inputs to this process include financial information such as targets, budget expenditure and realisation. Quality management may propose investments with financial impacts. Cost management may inform quality management of problems and opportunities for improvement with respect to costs and cost management. Service level management provides functional management with cost reports and other financial reports.

Operational processes. The impact analysis may show that changes impact the costs. The other processes can also provide information if there is any financial impact.

Finance department. The cost management process is closely related to the processes of the finance department. The finance department calculates cost prices, sets financial frameworks for the organisation, determines sales prices where relevant, raises invoices and monitors receivables. The results of these activities (information, invoices and indicators) provide input to cost management. Cost management provides invoicing information to the finance department.

7.4 Quality management

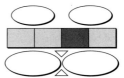

Objective
The objective of quality management is to assure the internal or external quality of the process and product by defining and monitoring this quality. Quality management includes the processes associated with application management quality management, e.g. by quality assurance of the ICT products, process management and monitoring the quality of the cooperation.

Issues
Quality management addresses four issues:
- The quality of the product: the quality of the application and documentation. Examples: software quality (structure, clarity), correctness, completeness and current relevance of the documentation.
- Quality of the production process: the quality of the structure of the processes, roles, responsibilities and procedures. Examples: unambiguous test and design procedures which all personnel are familiar with, the structure and quality of the processes, clear and agreed handover arrangements and clear agreements about tooling for application development.
- Quality of the quality system: the quality of the application development and application management infrastructure in the broader sense such as tools, methods and techniques. Examples: availability of a suitable development environment, supporting standard information with spreadsheets, and detailed test methods which also specify the tools.
- Quality of the organisation: personnel quality, expertise, place in the organisation, competencies, etc. Examples: adequate experience of tool X, adequate training facilities and knowledge management facilities, clear agreements with other parts of the organisation.

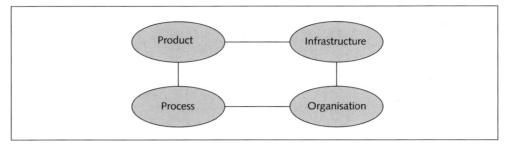

Figure 38 Quality management issues

These four issues are closely monitored by quality management. As discussed earlier in this chapter, monitoring means:
- Evaluating and looking back: did the releases progress as expected, is the maintenance and production process operating as expected, was the number of problems acceptable and are problems effectively resolved (see also the incident management process)?
- Verification: quality assurance, assessment on the basis of agreed standards, peer reviews, etc.
- Forecasting and making adjustments: do the experiences of strategic clusters suggest changes to the quality system or process, etc.?

Activities
Quality planning:
- assessing the required quality level and the current quality level;
- developing a quality plan with verifiable and feasible improvement measures, ambitions, required investments;
- initiating improvements to the quality system: developing guidelines for the tools, standards, methods, process flow and organisational structure.

Quality control:
- accepting and processing problems and proposals for improvement;
- regular assessment of the process, product, infrastructure and organisation, e.g. through audits, reviews and product and process assessments.

Quality review:
- evaluating the progress of releases, evaluation further to assurance efforts, reviews and assessments;
- evaluation of the overall quality of the product and process;
- evaluation of resolved problems.

Chapter 7 Management processes

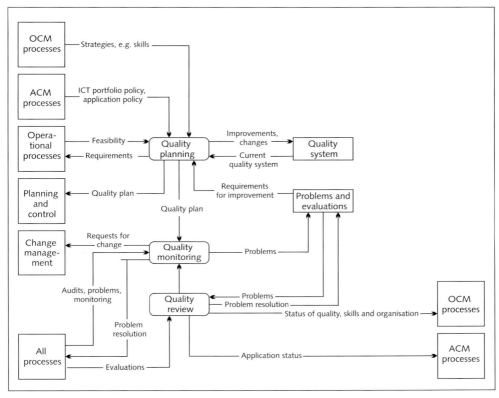

Figure 39 Quality management flow chart

Results

Quality system:
- tools for supporting the application management processes;
- methods for design, programming, etc.;
- techniques: development and test methodologies;
- tools: for development, testing and software configuration;
- manuals.

Quality plan:
- strategy;
- objectives;
- required improvements;
- activities and investments for the maintenance or improvement of the quality system (training plan, etc.).

Management plan (description of the organisation's production process):
- organisation, roles and responsibilities;
- activities/processes to be undertaken;
- tools, methods and techniques used;
- process requirements.

Problems, assessments and improvements:
- problems: status (outstanding or resolved), reported by, cause, measures, progress;
- product and process assessments and recommendations;
- suggested changes to the application or process;
- developments over time.

Relationships
Operational processes
The quality management process is responsible for providing the quality system to support and structure the application management processes. The methods and general requirements for processes and products are communicated to relevant personnel through quality management plans. The operational processes include evaluations which may result in identified problems and which provide input for quality control and review. Product assessments (audits) and tests provide information about the extent to which the planned quality level is fulfilled. The resolution of problems and changes to the quality system are communicated to the relevant processes.

Management processes
The management plan describes the required changes to the quality system. This plan, and the related investments, is submitted to planning and control. The requirements of service level management may necessitate improvements to the quality system. Improvements to the quality system are investments and may lead to increased costs, this information is provided to cost management.

OCM processes
Skills definition outlines a strategy for the way in which the organisation will provide it services in future. Thus, this process directs the expertise required by the organisation, and its knowledge management and quality systems. Consequently, this process largely determines the definition and updating of the quality system and the requirements made of it.

ACM processes
Quality management provides information about the status and quality (or lack thereof) of an application to life cycle management and ICT portfolio management. These processes develop a strategy for the applications and the objectives associated with these applications. The strategy may also lead to changes to the quality system and its underlying infrastructure.

7.5 Service level management

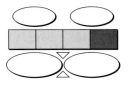

Objective
Service level management aims to monitor and improve customer satisfaction and to improve the services provided to the customer. This includes: defining the customer/supplier relationship, making and monitoring agreements between the customer and the application management organisation and updating these agreements. Service level management covers the activities needed to define the service level required by the customer, as well as monitoring the actual service level. The times at which the services are to be provided are determined in consultation with the customer.

Issues
Service levels are agreements about the process or result of the provision of services, described in terms which are clear to the customer, and which the application manager is committed to. Together, the service levels reflect the quality of service required by the customer. The full range of service levels is formally described in a Service Level Agreement (SLA) and associated contracts or assignments. The SLA is a document in which the customer and application manager agree the required level of service as well as the sanctions associated with failure to reach these levels.

Service levels can be broad and cover the following areas:
- The operation of the application. These agreements address the way in which the application works. Examples include performance, availability, future-proofing, internal quality of the application, etc.
- The functionality of the application. These agreements define what the application should do, now or in the next release.
- The service process. For example the time within which interruptions are addressed and resolved, time within which questions are answered, the number of bugs as a percentage of the size which may occur in a new version.
- The nature of the services provided by the application management organisation (service catalogue). The services provided by the organisation for which it is accountable, additional services and associated conditions, areas outside its accountability. The service package is the collection of services purchased by the customer.

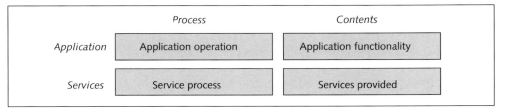

Figure 40 Service level management issues

SLAs have to be written most carefully. Service levels are subject to a number of requirements.

Scope of the service levels
As technical management has a longer history (due to ITIL, etc.) there is a tendency to largely consider service levels in terms of the first issue, i.e. the operation of the application. These agreements are often relatively technical and address the uptime, transaction times, etc. However, there are many other service levels within application management, which are often neglected.

Agreements about the functionality of the application are often implied as service levels although they are often explicitly monitored. The change management process and the acceptance test verify if the agreed changes are indeed realised in the required form. This is also a type of service level. Thus, the service level management process also monitors renovation processes.

The process by which the services are provided, as experienced by the customer, has a major impact on customer satisfaction and the appreciation of the application management organisation. This includes agreements about issues such as response time, feedback about the status of an incident or change, and clear communications if any limits are exceeded. The service boundaries and any changes to them should also be clearly defined and it should be clearly indicated if anything is outside the agreements or remit of the application management organisation. Thus, the service levels should cover all aspects of the services and should not be narrowly focussed on a few of the more technical processes.

Focus on results
The agreements should not describe the internal operations. Programming methods, tools, documentation methods, internal application management processes, etc. should not be included in the service levels. The requirements should be functional and focussed on the results, with the emphasis on the customer. The accountability, expertise and professionalism of the application manager will ensure that the results are indeed obtained. After all, if you buy a house you don't specify the grade of cement to be used, or how bricklayers should do their job.

Verifiable
Service levels should be verifiable (measurable) and reportable. Agreements should not include anything which will not be measured or cannot be measured. This means that every service level will require investments and capacity. Defining an appropriate set of service levels takes a great deal of attention and effort.

Appropriate: related to the needs
There is little point in agreeing service levels for issues of little relevance, as service levels equate to investments. It can be decided if a service level is appropriate by determining if the user organisation is inconvenienced if the agreed level is not reached.

Feasible
Service levels should be feasible. There is no point in agreeing service levels which cannot be met, at least not at present. The feasibility is essential, otherwise the SLA will simply be a paper tiger. This means that developing an achievable and feasible service level takes a significant amount of time and may require a transition period. It is not unusual to start with a pilot period and then aim for a feasible level.

Dependencies
When drawing up a service level the customer and supplier have to be aware that they may be dependent on other organisations (subcontractors, facility providers). If they want to be responsible for realising a service level then they will have to take management action. If there is little management action directed at other organisations it is debatable if agreements about the services as a whole will be effective.

Changes in service levels
Needs and requirements change over time. The needs may change greatly over a period of several years. These changes relate to the environment and the customer's market (they may have to operate more flexibly on the market). Needs may also change because set objectives are attained. The need for cost control often inspires more professional application management. After some time, the customer gets used to controllable and reliable costs, and this becomes an expectation. After that, the customer may develop a need for quality improvements or more flexibility. If the application management organisation cannot respond appropriately, tensions are likely to occur.

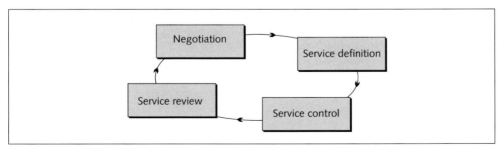

Figure 41 Steps within service level management

ASL A Framework for Application Management

Activities
Service level management has a similar division into stages as the other management processes.

Service definition – identifying and refining agreements and service levels:
- identifying customer needs or updating needs;
- determining the relevance, feasibility and desirability of a need: determining its relevance, impact on services (cost of providing the service level) and investments for its internal introduction (process design);
- clearly defining needs in agreements: drafting the SLA, possibly as an annex to a contract;
- operational introduction: setting up the organisation and implementing the instruments to measure and report service levels;

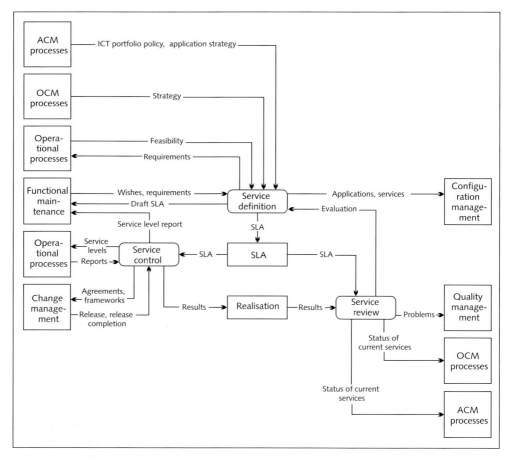

Figure 42 Service level management flowchart

- introduction: making the service levels effective;
- definition: defining the required values.

Service control – monitoring and updating:
- measuring the service levels;
- reporting on service levels;
- estimating the risk that service levels are not fulfilled or have little relevance;
- taking measures to reach the desired situation.

Service review – evaluation:
- evaluating the actual service levels and values;
- identifying opportunities for improvement;
- identifying the lessons learned;
- identifying problems and improvement measures.

Results
Contract/SLA:
- contract/form of contract (parties, form of the services, liability, rates);
- service catalogue (standard and additional services);
- agreed service levels;
- agreements about the services to be provided;
- service objects (applications);
- changes to service objects (changes to the application).

Realisation:
- service levels;
- service level realisation (over time).

Service report:
- agreed service levels;
- service level realisation;
- trends.

Information about the services to customers/users and strategic processes:
- current services;
- current customers and agreements.

Relationships
Operational processes
Obviously, there are clear relationships with the maintenance and enhancement processes as most of the service levels will apply to them. These processes provide reports and data about the agreed service levels. The primary sources of information are incident

management, continuity management, availability management, change management and implementation. The agreements about the applications and services to be provided are communicated to configuration management.

Other management processes
There are also relationships with the management processes:
- investments, capacity, etc. (planning and control);
- service catalogue tasks and responsibilities (quality management);
- problems and proposals for improvement (quality management) to meet the service levels or agreements made with the customer.

There is an essential difference between the service level management process and quality management. Quality covers everything which has not been agreed with the customer but which is nevertheless relevant to the future or the provision of services. This means that quality management is concerned with appropriate and effective application management. Quality management also takes a long-term approach.

Everything agreed with the customer (even if it is not included in good application management) is covered by service level management. Consequently, service level management takes and external approach.

OCM processes
Service level management provides information about the current services and agreements to account definition and service delivery definition. These processes provide the strategy towards customers, new customers and any new services. All this provides input to service level management.

ACM processes
Life cycle management and ICT portfolio management provide plans for renovation and the ICT portfolio policies. These not only include agreements and policies (expectations) about the long-term future of the applications, but also result in new service requirements. These processes are provided with information about the current agreements, services, trends, and the extent to which the current agreements can be fulfilled. The service level management process can also provide information about developments in the user organisation to the customer organisation strategy process.

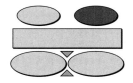

CHAPTER 8

Applications Cycle Management (ACM)

The ASL messages
— Innovation and renewal of the business processes will increasingly be based on current applications because businesses will no longer invest in full scale redevelopment.
— Application portfolio management is becoming an essential issue in application management.
— Information about developments in the user organisation, user organisation environment, and technical environment will determine the interface with the business processes.

8.1 Introduction

Objectives and background
ACM, Applications Cycle Management, is concerned with the future supply of information, the lifecycle of objects (applications). This occurs at two levels: the individual application level, and the application portfolio level. This process addresses the coming three to five years and develops strategies and actions for improvement for a similar or slightly longer period.

Innovation is increasingly based on the current situation
The hectic situation on the market and within organisations makes it difficult to get a clear view of the long-term (e.g. ten years) requirements. Organisations, mergers, joint ventures, and new products follow in quick succession. It is impossible to outline what the organisation will be in ten years, and to determine what will be important at that time.

Deciding about a new information system for a large organisation, and designing and developing it can take four to five years. The quality of the new information system is determined in part by the extent to which it matches developments after its handover, i.e. the following five or ten years. It is therefore extremely difficult to design future-proof information systems as it is likely to require a view of the next decade.

All of this means that it is extremely difficult to come up with a completely new design for the ICT infrastructure of a large information-intensive organisation. Furthermore, most of the new applications will largely offer the same functions as those they replace. It may therefore be more effective to focus on incremental steps, improving current applications and allowing them to develop into the required new situation. Application management must proactively consider the future of applications.

Portfolio management
It is becoming increasingly apparent that the development of a completely new information system is unmanageable, both in terms of the management and the users. Many organisations can no longer cope with a complete change in the organisation, business processes, culture, methods and users. After all, the business processes have to continue. Consequently, change management will increasingly develop into managing changes to elements of the organisation. This means that a portfolio approach is becoming more important.

The long-term view
Within application management, the long-term view is becoming essential: application management will have to become aware that the current applications will determine the competitive strength of the user organisation for the next five years. Traditionally, application management has not been good at taking a long-term view. It requires a conscious consideration of developments in the application management environment.

Issues
To anticipate the future we have to understand the developments in the application environment. We need to watch the trends in technology, the environment and chain, and the user organisation.

ACM includes three processes to provide this information:
1. ICT developments strategy monitors and assesses new developments in technology.
2. Customer environment strategy obtains information about developments in the user organisation environment in relation to the application(s).
3. Customer organisation strategy identifies developments in the user organisation.

The internal condition of the applications (quality and cost) can also necessitate significant changes to the applications. This requires strategies at two levels:
1. Life cycle management is the process which defines a strategy for the future of the application, in terms of actions.
2. ICT portfolio management is the process which determines the strategy for the applications and provision of information as a whole.

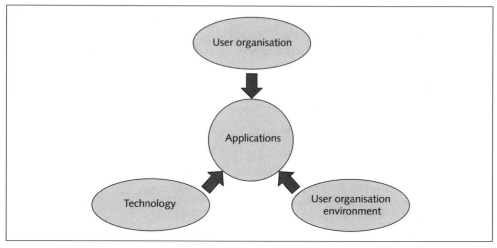

Figure 43 Issues in ACM

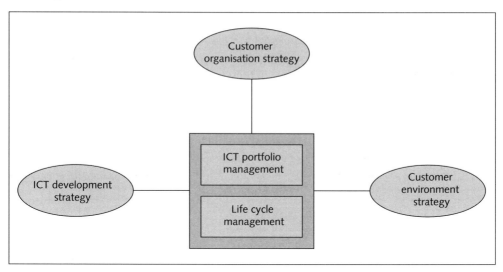

Figure 44 ACM processes

Relationships with other forms of maintenance
Within application management, the ACM processes tend to approach issues from the perspective of the application. However, there are also other approaches, based on the infrastructure (technical management) or provision of information (functional management). Clearly, these approaches are also essential when determining the future direction. The views from the three different perspectives are combined with developing the overall strategy.

8.2 ICT developments strategy

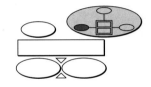

Objective
The ICT developments strategy is the process which monitors and reviews new developments in technology. The process identifies ICT developments which may be relevant to the organisation and its information supply. The most important developments will be in applications development technology (development and management/maintenance tools), but new infrastructure (networking, audio, video) may also create opportunities with a major impact on the applications. Developments can also lead to risks, for example to continuity. The objective of ICT developments strategy is to determine the impact of technical developments on the application portfolio.

Issues
The ICT developments strategy process is not limited to trends in application development and enhancement such as development environments and developments in ERP. IT developments can also have a significant impact on the long-term future of applications. Infrastructure developments are also relevant, although the development of a strategy for this area is primarily the responsibility of other maintenance processes. The impact of developments in ICT on applications is so significant that the ICT developments strategy operates in close conjunction with the similar processes in technical management and functional management.

Technology deployment involves a number of issues:
1. The plans of a supplier for their product are important. Plans to wind-down or end support for releases affect the application. This may lead to forced migrations.
2. New releases or products may offer additional functions. These may provide an option for solving any problems in the current provision of information.
3. Developments among the customers and users of these products are also relevant, particularly with respect to continuity and support. It can be a disadvantage to be the only user of a package, for example where future support is concerned.
4. But this may also have advantages, it is easier to influence the functionality of a package if you are one of only a few users.

Thus, these developments may pose both threats and opportunities. Four types of technology are relevant in this context, and each has a different impact on the applications. The first two issues are the remit of technical management:
- Infrastructure is the entirety of hardware components used, including network technology, etc.
- System software is software which runs on the hardware and provides the basic functions for system development, maintenance, enhancement and operations. System software is

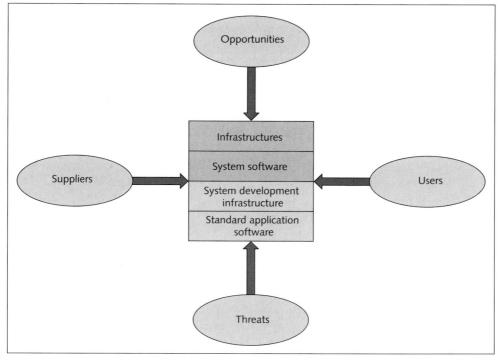

Figure 45 Issues in IT development

an essential link between the hardware and the other software. It includes database management systems, operating systems, etc.

There are two types of software which are the direct responsibility of application management:
- System development infrastructure is the entirety of tools used to build, maintain and enhance applications. This includes compilers, programming environments, database management environments, documentation environments and CASE tools, software distribution systems, etc. These tools are used to develop and enhance applications.
- Standard software is software developed and enhanced by third parties whose functions are fixed (within certain limits) and can be used within an application. Examples include ERP packages, components or objects and ASP-type functions.

Activities
Survey:
- identifying technical developments relevant to the business processes which the applications as a whole relate to;

- identifying the needs for their introduction and the opportunities provided by the new technology;
- selecting potentially attractive technology and obtaining further information about its value, such as costs, compatibility, risks, investments, options for future development.

Impact assessment:
- charting a general technology strategy or direction;
- identifying the impact on the current applications portfolio.

Results
Technology strategy:
- attractive opportunities or the need for new technology, potential application, advantages and risks;
- technology strategy plan;
- logical progression from the current technology.

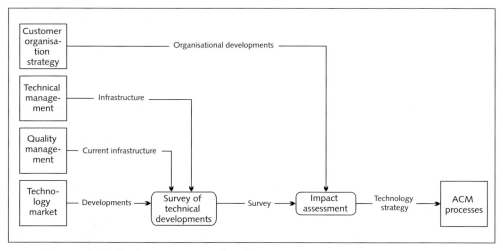

Figure 46 ICT developments strategy flowchart

Relationships
Technical management
Technical management has a wealth of knowledge about developments in infrastructure and their impact on the applications, which can be applied in this process.

Other ACM processes
This process provides input for the ICT portfolio management and life cycle management processes.

OCM processes
This process addresses the same issues as technology definition within OCM. Although there is no formal relationship it may be useful to reuse appropriate results.

8.3 Customer environment strategy

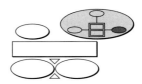

Objective
Organisations increasingly operate as links in a chain of organisations. In terms of the provision of information this creates strong dependencies between organisations and the applications of other organisations. The options an organisation has for the provision of information determine, in part, its place in these chains. The applications in the surrounding environment and their development are therefore becoming increasingly important in application management. Customer environment strategy addresses developments in the provision of information and data exchange between organisations (chain management) and provides information about the requirements and opportunities in terms of the provision of information to the user organisation. The objective of customer environment strategy is to determine the impact of developments in the environment surrounding the user organisation on the application portfolio.

Issues
Process chains focus on communications between and the integration of organisations. We can identify the following levels of communications and integration:
- The business processes of the organisations: what steps comprise the chain, and what are the relationships between the steps across the organisations (i.e. which step in the chain is covered by what organisation).
- What information flows can we identify between the processes (process steps) and organisations (what information or operations are exchanged).
- What automated data or functions does the information exchange relate to, and what systems provide functions and data and how is it defined (specification, format, syntax).
- What infrastructure components are needed for the integration, and which components are available. Examples include networks, security aspects, middleware and protocols.

When exchanging information we should not only consider the requirements (organisational processes → information flow → data and functions → infrastructure), but also the supply. What are the options provided by the infrastructure, data, functions, etc. to facilitate integration and optimisation?

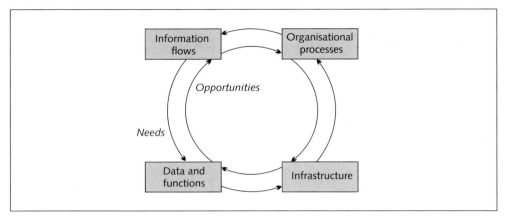

Figure 47 Issues in customer environment strategy

Activities
Survey:
- identifying relevant developments in the business processes across the organisations, including customers of the user organisation (chain processes) and the need to automate these;
- identifying the flow of information and information processing which is currently carried or required for these chain processes, and identifying the relevant data, systems and programs;
- identifying and selecting the potential or essential communications infrastructure such as middleware, networks, etc.

Impact assessment:
- defining the general strategy or direction of the processes in the chain and their development;
- identifying the options for developing potentially relevant chain processes on the basis of the current infrastructure and applications.

Results
Developments based on processes in the chain:
- changes required by the chain/column approach;
- impact on business processes and underlying applications;
- changes in the user organisation and surrounding environment of the user organisation;
- attractive options for integration or data exchange;
- require changes in the management of the provision of information.

Chapter 8   Applications Cycle Management

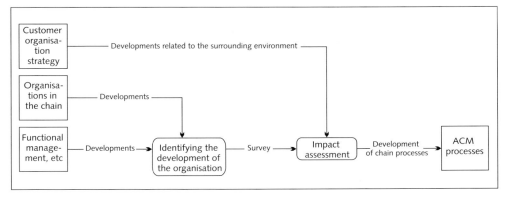

Figure 48 Customer environment strategy flowchart

Relationships
Functional management, organisations in the chain
The information for this process is obtained from the organisations in the chain (information suppliers and customers) and from functional management.

OCM processes
The implementation of this process is focussed on the ICT portfolio management and life cycle management processes. The results of this process can also provide input to the other ACM processes, such as customer organisation strategy. Furthermore, the results can also be relevant input for the business strategies of the organisations in the chain.

8.4   Customer organisation strategy

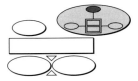

Objectives
Apart from developments in the surrounding environment, internal developments in the user organisation are obviously also most important. Customer organisation strategy is the process which monitors developments in the user organisation. It determines proactively what the impact on the applications will be, what impediments the applications form to these developments, and how we should respond to these impediments. The objective is to determine the impact of developments in the user organisation on the application portfolio.

Issues
The customer organisation strategy process aims to understand developments within the user organisation, but not to define actions further to these developments. The actions further to these developments are taken within the life cycle management and ICT

117

portfolio management processes. The identification of these developments may bridge a number of renovation processes.

This process also meets the need for structured information about the user organisation (developing and maintaining expertise about this specific issue) and changes in the user organisation. This process also identifies where activities could be incorporated in the ICT portfolio. The approach of this process is purely based on the user organisation.

Issues relevant to this process include:
- business processes;
- customers of the customer/user organisation;
- customer's suppliers;
- infrastructure;
- organisational structure (structure, finance, personnel);
- changes in IT management.

Figure 49 shows these issues and their structure. Appropriate methods and models for these activities include the strategy impact gauge, Lamp and SSP.

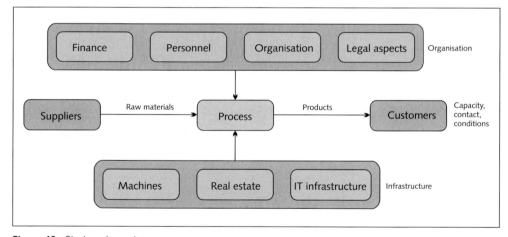

Figure 49 Strategy impact gauge

Activities

Survey:
- identifying changes in strategy;
- identifying changes in the business process (including customers and suppliers);
- identifying the infrastructure;

- identifying changes in the nature of the organisation (changes in the organisational structure, accountability, financial standards, personnel issues);
- identifying changes in ICT management.

Impact assessment:
- identifying the applications affected by the developments;
- identifying the blanks in the support of the business process by the current information systems;
- identifying the impact, in outlines, on current and potential future information systems.

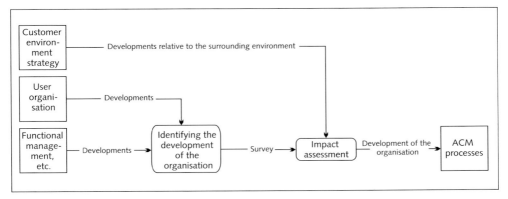

Figure 50 Customer organisation strategy flowchart

Results
Development of the organisation and impact on the applications:
- changes in the business process, organisation and management of the provision of information;
- impact on applications (which applications, and to what extent are they affected by developments).

Relationships
Functional management, user organisation
Much of the information is provided by functional management and the user organisation and its management.

ACM processes
The output of this process is used by the ICT portfolio management and life cycle management processes. The results of this process can also provide input for the OCM processes. Input for this process may also be provided by service level management.

8.5 Life cycle management

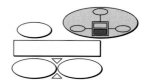

Objective
Life cycle management aims to set out a strategy for the future of an application, defined in actions, to ensure that the application will provide the best possible support to the business processes over the next few years.

As discussed in section 8.1.1, applications now have much longer lives than ever expected, and their lifespan will actually increase in future. Furthermore the demand will increasingly be for replacement rather than new IT systems.

In practice, it is also becoming more common to replace parts of applications which makes the distinction between old and new systems less clear. Hence, the ASL philosophy is that application management amounts to supporting the business processes during their lifetime by information systems (instead of maintaining and enhancing an information system during its lifetime). This means that the emphasis shifts from the system to the business process.

Consequently, the long-term perspectives of an application are particularly important. The logical choice is to take the current situation as the starting point for the future.

The life cycle management (LCM) process matches the current options and future requirements and develops the strategy to move from the one to the other. The life cycle management process usually operates on the level of one application (or a few closely related applications) and is therefore more detailed and more substantive, and more closely focussed on the specific business process than the ICT portfolio management process. The substantive development of this process could be based on B-IS-A, see Figure 51. However, there are also other suitable options, and ASL does not specify any particular approach.

Issues
The following issues determine the development of the strategy for the future:
- the current quality of the application in the broader sense (functional, technical and operational quality);
- the required changes further to changes in the surrounding environment, developments in the organisation, and strategy;
- the technical options;
- potential renovation scenarios and outlines;

Chapter 8 Applications Cycle Management

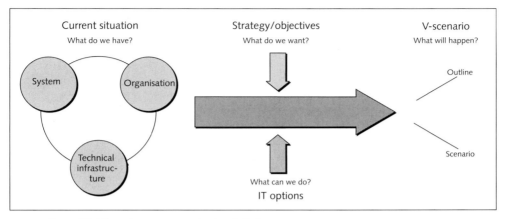

Figure 51 Life cycle management using B-IS-A

Activities

Status of the current situation:
- determining the quality of the application perceived by the user (fit with the business process, ergonomics, information quality, cost);
- determining the technical quality and ease of enhancement;
- ease of operation and operational quality of the application.

Outlining the strategy:
- with respect to developments and changes originating in the business process, strategy, surrounding environment;
- with respect to the detailed impact on applications.

Identifying technical options:
- identifying relevant or essential technology;
- determining its deployability and value to the application.

Defining the strategy:
- drawing up potential scenarios and outlines;
- determining investments, benefits, advantages, disadvantages, extent to which the requirements are fulfilled;
- recommendation/choice of scenario.

Results

Application strategy:
- status of the current application (strengths and weaknesses in use, operation and enhancement);

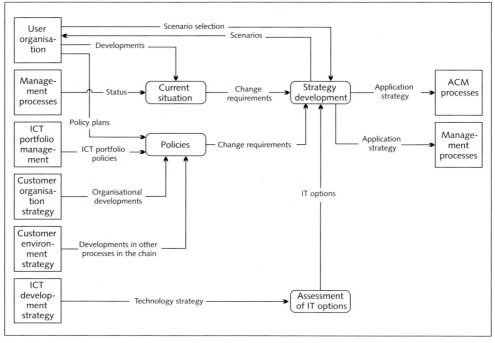

Figure 52 Life cycle management flowchart

- developments: desirable or required changes based on the surrounding environment or strategy;
- enhancement scenarios, outlines and considerations (potential architectures and scenarios, advantages and disadvantages of the scenarios;
- long-term application strategy (structural improvement, plans and schedules, investments);
- short-term improvements (quick wins).

Relationships
Other ACM processes
Life cycle management receives some of its input from processes which monitor developments in the surrounding environment. These are: customer organisation strategy, customer environment strategy, and ICT developments strategy. The strategy for an application should correspond to the outlines of the portfolio.

Management processes
The management processes such as planning and control, service level management, and most of all, quality management, provide information about various aspects of the appli-

cation, such as its quality (ease of technical enhancement), problems, scope and cost of applications, service levels and the extent to which they are achieved.

Functional management
Functional management provides detailed information about the use of the applications and the business processes. It also selects the strategy which will eventually be adopted. For this reasons, the scenarios are communicated back to functional management.

8.6   ICT portfolio management

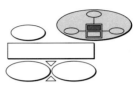

Objective
ICT portfolio management aims to optimise the coordination of larger investments and changes in objects used for the provision of information. The process identifies the significance and performance of applications with respect to the user organisation, interprets the business strategy for objects used for the provision of information, and uses this to define a strategy for the future of the objects in the ICT portfolio, considering the connections between the objects.

Issues
Life cycle management sets the strategy for a single application, while ICT portfolio management covers the whole range of applications. The emphasis in this process lies on the coherence and coordinating actions affecting different objects (applications). The activities in this process are similar to those covered by information policy or information planning.

In application management, the whole spectrum covered by the ICT portfolio is too broad a concept. Application management is primarily concerned with applications. Such a study is undertaken together with functional management and technical management, and ASL is primarily focussed on managing the application portfolio. Examples of relevant issues are given in Figure 53 which is based on the New Information Planning (NIP) method. NIP is an example of an appropriate method, alternatives include MAIA and ISP. ASL does not specify any particular method.

Activities
We propose that ICT portfolio management should include the activities which are also covered by the life cycle management process:
- identifying the current status of the ICT portfolio: current quality of the ICT portfolio in the broader sense (strengths/weaknesses, functional quality, technical quality, operational quality);

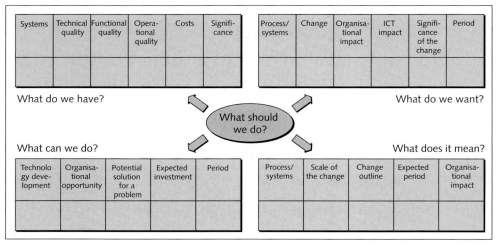

Figure 53 Issues in ICT portfolio management

- identifying desirable changes further to developments in the surrounding environment, organisation and strategy;
- identifying the applicability of new technical options;
- defining the strategy and activities to bring about the desired ICT portfolio: initiating special activities to introduce changes and renovation or including them in the routine application management process.

Results
ICT portfolio status:
- status, strengths and weaknesses of the applications;
- strategy, developments and impact on applications;
- technical options;
- desired change (nature of the project, accountability, etc.).

ICT portfolio management:
- activities, actors, nature of the actions;
- strategy outlines;
- planned actions and expected investments.

Relationships
Other ACM processes
Organisation environment strategy, customer organisation strategy and ICT developments strategy are all processes which provide information abut the developments in the user organisation environment, the user organisation itself, and in information technology. Consequently these processes provide input for the steps in this process.

Chapter 8 Applications Cycle Management

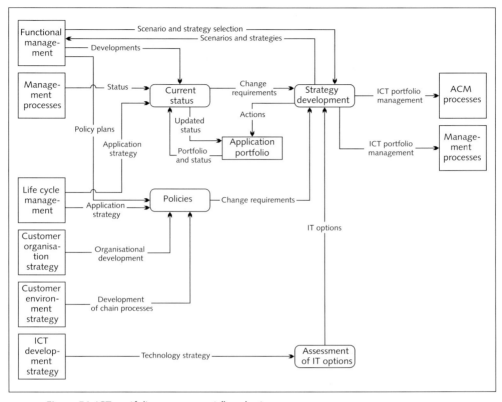

Figure 54 ICT portfolio management flowchart

Life cycle management
Life cycle management sets the strategy for a single application in the application portfolio. A strategy set by life cycle management is more detailed, developed to a greater extent and provides more substantive information about the renovation strategy. Of course, the strategy has to fit in with the portfolio. Depending on the sequence of the processes (which depends on the way the provision of information is managed) the information will be exchanged concurrently or before or after each process.

Management processes
The management processes such as planning and control, service level management and especially quality management provide information about aspects of the applications, such as quality (ease of technical enhancement), problems, scale and cost of applications, services provided, and the extent to which the service levels are realised.

Functional management

Functional management includes similar processes which primarily provide details about the provision of information. The scenarios and strategies are communicated to the other processes. The final decision about the strategy is taken by functional management.

CHAPTER 9

Organisation Cycle Management (OCM)

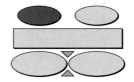

The ASL messages
— Application management organisations have to take a proactive stance to the future and the services to be provided.
— The difference between internal and external application management organisations will reduce. The demands made of both types will become increasingly similar.
— Application management organisations will have to consider the role they want to play, and which partners they want to cooperate with.
— The strategy to be pursued first has to be developed bottom-up and then top-down.

9.1 Introduction

Objectives and background
Organisation Cycle Management (OCM) is the cluster of processes which define the future of the services and structure of the application management organisation. This cluster of processes forms an essential element of ASL.

This cluster is important for a number of reasons:
- The relationships between the application manager, application and user organisation are no longer cast in stone.
- Application management organisations are often conservative and little aware of future developments. As a result they may lose touch with the user organisation and their issues.
- The services demanded by the users become so broad that it is difficult for internal or external application management organisations to provide the full range. This necessitates a decision about the services which should be provided by the internal application management organisation and those where a partnership might be appropriate. The role of the application management organisation in such a partnership should also be considered.

- The strategy of the application management organisation should clearly consider the current services and initiate an evolution in the range of services provided.

Relationships between the user organisation, application and application manager
Application management is normally very stable as most applications are managed and enhanced for a period of years. However, the application management market is no longer static. Trends such as outsourcing or splitting service departments off as independent businesses mean that user organisations are no longer always required to deal with the internal application management organisation.

Internal suppliers increasingly have to meet the same standards as external suppliers
Increasingly, application management organisations are expected to charge market rates. Some user organisations select a new application management organisation further to technical developments such as ERP and ASP. Developments such as ASP not only have a significant impact on the user organisation, but even more on the application management function. This means that in our thinking we have to separate the application management organisation from the ICT portfolio it manages.

Innovation in application management
Application management organisations are often conservative in their operations, standards and values. Application management organisations find it difficult to deal with changing demands for services ("that's impossible", "we can't do that"). This often encourages trends such as outsourcing. Consequently, application management organisations should give more consideration to their future, organisation, services they want to offer, and the market they want to supply. This issues are addressed by the organisations cycle management cluster (OCM).

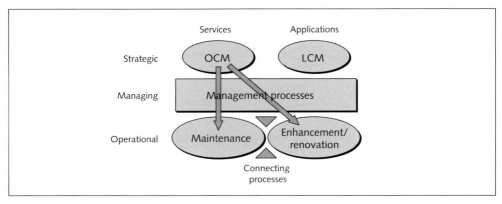

Figure 55 OCM services

Innovation in services

OCM defines the strategy taken by the service organisation. This cluster of processes sets the strategy to ensure that the required service level is provided in the long term and that appropriate services are developed, to maintain or replace the customer base. In other words: what is our future service portfolio and how can we provide it? This should cover all services, including those related to the enhancement and renovation processes.

Issues

There are four issues relevant to the considerations about future services:
- The market: developments among customers, customer groups, other suppliers on the market, needs, demand.
- The current customer base, the accounts: relationships and contacts between our organisation and our current customers.
- The technology: developments on the market which can be deployed for customers.
- Skills/expertise: the people and instruments in our organisation which serve the customers. Alternative terms include competency and capability: the ability to deliver services.

These issues address:
- Demand vs. supply.
- The distinction between what the surrounding environment sends to the organisation, and what the application management organisation sends to the environment.

The strategic processes eventually result in a strategy: the services which the application management organisation wants to provide in about two or three years. The strategy is developed in five processes:
- Market definition (environment or market we want to operate in): process to identify the developments in the market and the position of our application management organisation in it. This includes considerations such as the developments in the market, other parties on the market, parties we can cooperate with, current/future elements of the market we can provide services to, and the parties we will be working with (analysis of the competition, forming alliances).
- Account definition (who to): the process to determine how the services are delivered to the customers, how the demand is recognised, and our position as a service provider on the market. What do our current customers want? What new services should we provide, how, who to and presenting what image?
- Skills definition (capacity, skills, knowledge assessment – how): determining the strategy to develop the required knowledge and expertise (capabilities) in the organisation. What skills and expertise do we need? Which have to be acquired or developed? How will we do this in future?
- Technology definition (what with): determining the strategy for tools, methods, development methodologies, etc. to be followed, acquired and used in the near future.

- Service delivery definition (what): defining the services to be provided and determining the outline strategy to provide them.

Obviously, these issues closely resemble the normal strategic considerations.

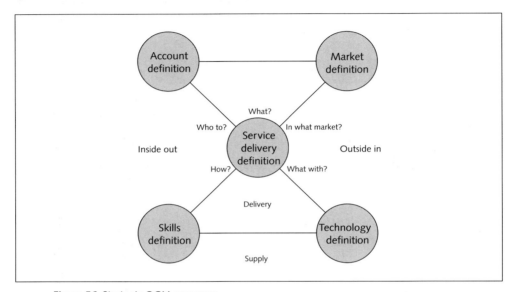

Figure 56 Strategic OCM processes

Approach
The strategic processes deliver two products:
- definition of the ambitions: the goals;
- strategy: how to reach the goals.

The names of the processes clearly indicate the definition aspect, which logically leads to the strategy. The steps connecting these processes are shown in Figure 57. The first step is to identify the relevant areas. This leads to a SWOT analysis with opportunities and threats associated with the different elements (e.g. technology, market). The results from these areas are combined in the service delivery definition process. This coordinates the processes and defines the goals for the services to be provided in two years, and their dependencies. These goals are then detailed in the relevant processes and lead to a strategy which is then communicated.

Chapter 9 Organisation Cycle Management

Internal service providers – external service providers
OCM might appear to be relevant only to external service providers. However, this assumption is incorrect. Internal service providers in particular have to be aware of their position in the organisation, requirements from the user organisation, services they want to continue to provide in-house, and the services for which they will enter a partnership with external organisations. This is essential to continue to ensure the effective support of the customer's business processes.

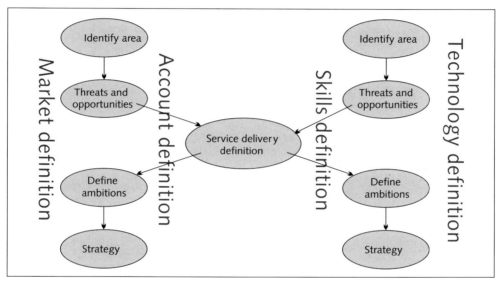

Figure 57 OCM processes

Relationships with ACM processes
The processes within applications cycle management relate to the strategy for the information management of the user organisation. Normally, the user organisation is responsible for the outcome of the ACM processes. (The situation may be different when package suppliers or ASP service providers are used.) ACM boils down to: what does the customer want to do with the applications? OCM means: what can our service organisation do? There are normally differences between the two answers. Consequently, the processes have no formal relationship with the OCM processes and do not officially exchange information. These processes only meet in the stage 'chain oriented' of the EFQM model. However, it is advisable to be aware of the outcome of the ACM processes and use them for the definition steps in OCM.

9.2 Market definition

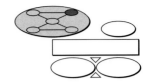

Objective
Market definition is the process of analysing developments in the market and among the customers, and determining which elements of the market are relevant to the services to be provided. The objective of this process is to define and detail the envisaged position of the application management organisation in its environment, and to set up the cooperation required to provide the appropriate services.

User organisations operate in a rapidly changing environment. In certain sectors (e.g. energy and finance) there is a strong trend towards acquisitions, mergers, globalisation, and targeting a specific part of the market. These trends have a major impact on application management and the organisation which provides it to the user organisation. In all these turbulent developments, the position f the application management organisation is of secondary interest to the user organisation. After a merger the most effective ICT organisation will often take the lead.

Issues
The market definition process defines developments and trends in the provision of services so we can determine the customer groups and requirements which will be relevant to application management services in future. In essence, we determine our position in the future market.

Relevant issues include:
- what products and potential substitutes will be available on the market to these customers groups (e.g. ERP for bespoke systems, ASP, Internet developments);
- what potential competition is there, and what is their effect on existing agreements and positions;
- what is the position and bargaining power of suppliers and buyers and which services could be taken over;
- what potential new entrants (competition) will there be;
- what potential new market segments will there be?

The Porter model can be used as a guideline. Potential forms of cooperation or joint ventures are also relevant. In the current market, only few organisations can provide the full range of services.

Activities
Market survey:
- identifying developments among user organisations which operate in similar areas as the current customer groups;

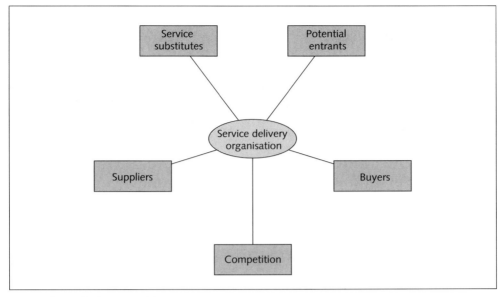

Figure 58 Porter model

- identifying service developments in this broader market;
- identifying developments in technology and substitute products in this broader market (ASP, e-commerce);
- identifying competitors and potential partners.

Defining threats and opportunities:
- defining threats and opportunities in current and new markets;
- defining threats and opportunities for services.

Market definition:
- defining attractive prospective customers or customer groups;
- defining attractive services for new customers;
- defining attractive forms of cooperation with other organisations.

Developing the market strategy:
- scenarios to tap new markets;
- scenarios to develop cooperation.

Results
Market survey:
- identification of developments on the market;
- threats and opportunities (SWOT).

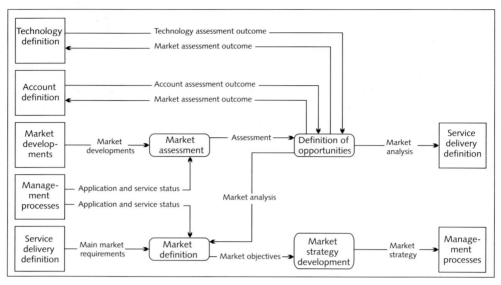

Figure 59 Market definition flowchart

Market strategy:
- envisaged position on the market;
- measures and strategy to enter any new markets.

Relationships
OCM processes
Account definition provides information about developments among current customers, in so far as these concern the services. This information can be used to verify conclusions drawn by the market definition process. Account definition is informed of the outlines of the developments observed by market definition. There is a similar relationship with the technology definition process. Market definition also provides input to the service delivery definition. The results from the survey provide input for the service delivery definition process. Service delivery definition provides the main objectives which are then developed in greater detail within the market definition process.

Management processes
The outcome of the market definition process (strategy and objectives) provides input for the management processes.

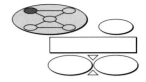

9.3 Account definition

Objective

Account definition is the process of determining the strategy and approach for contacting prospective customers. This relates to the intended image, presentation, vision and implementation in the working methods and organisation. Thus, the objective of account definition is to define and detail the relationship with the user organisation(s).

Issues

Important issues in this process include:
- image: the impression the application management and its services make on the customers;
- relationships: contact persons and contact facilities of the application management organisation within the user organisation;
- account organisation: personnel who inform the user organisation of the services available and who manage the services in terms of the relationship;
- product/service catalogue: services available and provided and the performance of the application management organisation (see also service level management).

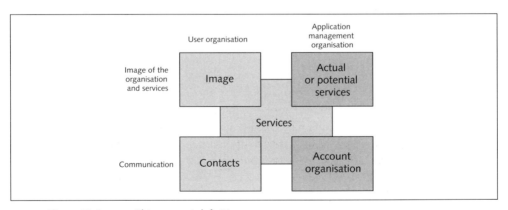

Figure 60 Issues within account definition

Activities

Defining the current position:
- identifying the image (impression the application management organisation makes);
- identifying contacts and channels with the current customers, including the service portfolio provided to the user organisation;
- identifying developments affecting customers, in terms of services and technology;

- identifying the status of our relationship network and contacts with our customers and any other groups.

Defining threats and opportunities:
- identifying opportunities for providing additional services to current customers;
- identifying threats to the current services and end of life cycle services;
- matching the results among the customer base with the outcome of the market definition process.

Defining services and the account:
- defining the required services, services to current customers, and future services;
- defining these services and the associated vision in greater detail.

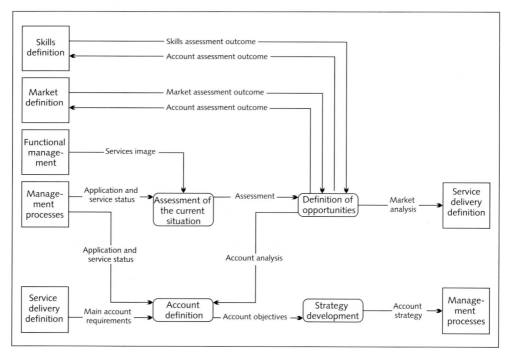

Figure 61 Account definition flowchart

Determining the account strategy:
- determining the desirable and required contacts;
- determining the services to be provided to the user organisation or parts thereof in greater detail;

- determining the activities and means to implement the desired situation (in terms of contacts and image).

Results
Account survey:
- survey of the customers and image, current customer contacts, internal contact persons, services provided;
- threats and opportunities (SWOT) with respect to current customers and services.

Objectives and account strategy:
- objectives and customer action plan, account objectives, desired image, desired services, desired contacts in the user/customer organisation;
- measures and investment in the external account organisation, relationships, image and external communications.

Relationships
OCM
The outcome of the survey provides input to the service delivery definition process. This process then provides the general objectives which are developed in greater detail in the following two steps in account definition. During the survey, information is exchanged with the market definition and skills definition processes.

Management processes
Service level management and planning and control are the two management processes with the strongest links with account definition. Service level management provides information about the services currently provided (service catalogue), performance and customers. Planning and control provides information about the scale of the services provided. The strategy defined by account definition provides input for these management processes.

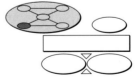

9.4 Skills definition

Objective
Skills definition is the process of defining the skills and expertise needed in the future. This concerns not only the depth, but also the scope and distribution and knowledge management. Thus, skills definition is the process which set objectives and gives direction to the capabilities of the application management organisation. The previous two processes defined the needs and possibilities associated with the environment. These have to be met by skills with the required scope and depth. Hence, we need objectives and a strategy to develop and deploy the skills, depth of the expertise, and scope of the

skills in the application management organisation, i.e. on the supply side. The current skills may actually stand in the way of the market and service objectives. The ambitions should be feasible, and there should be a link to the present situation.   Furthermore, the current expertise, which is sometimes limited or hidden in an organisation, may offer additional opportunities on the market. This means that an understanding of the current situation is important to the strategy.

Issues

The issues covered by skills definition include:
- The resources the organisation is or will have to be familiar with to provide the required services, and the demands they make on the current situation.
- The quality system (see quality management): how is the use of these resources supported, in what direction should the product and process quality develop?
- Experience of the organisation: how much experience is there and what is its depth? How many experts are there, in what areas, what is the depth of their expertise in these areas?
- The knowledge management system. How are the experience and expertise broadened within the organisation? This may also be considered to form part of quality management. Knowledge management also covers less visible activities such as coaching, support, knowledge dissemination and culture.

The issues in this process have clear links with the quality management (first and second issues) and planning and control (third and fourth issues) processes.

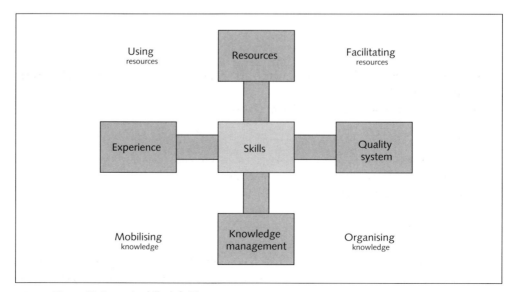

Figure 62 Issues in skills definition

Activities

Describing the current situation:
- defining the internal quality system (internal tools and instruments) and innovation in this area;
- identifying the skills, scope and depth of the expertise in the organisation with respect to the services;
- identifying the deployment and depth of the expertise;
- identifying the current knowledge management system (internal instruments for knowledge dissemination and training) and required improvement.

Identifying threats and opportunities:
- identifying requirements and threats related to skills, knowledge and experience;
- identifying the opportunities to market any of these.

Skills definition:
- more detailed definition of the objectives and ambitions as defined in the service delivery definition process.

Developing a strategy to implement the objectives:
- defining knowledge management measures;
- identifying the approach to develop the skills to the required scope and depth (through the training strategy and/or recruitment policies);
- identifying investments and measures related to the quality system and improvements in knowledge management.

Results

Survey:
- scope and depth of the current expertise and skills, status of the current quality system and organisation;
- threats and opportunities related to these issues.

Strategy:
- quality strategy and competency strategy for the coming years;
- quantitative objectives for experience and skills;
- measures and actions to meet these objectives.

Relationships

Management processes

The skills definition process has a close relationship with the management processes as the strategy is primarily focused on our own organisation. Quality management and planning and control provide input about the current situation (expertise, quantities,

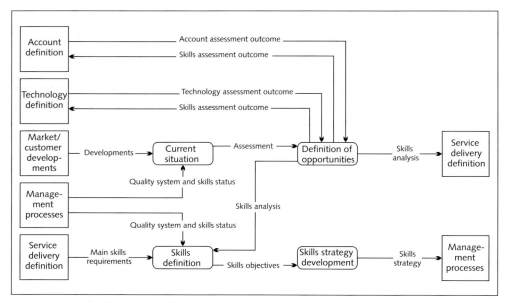

Figure 63 Skills definition flowchart

competencies, current skills and technology). Service level management provides information about the demand and demand trends. The outcome of the skills definition process (objectives and strategy) will largely have to be implemented through management action based on quality management and planning and control.

OCM

There is a strong connection between the technology definition and skills definition processes. The objective of skills definition is to identify the technology which will be used, and how the technology can be incorporated in the organisation's quality system. Technology definition is primarily concerned with external aspects. Actions in this area aim to develop knowledge and experience which is not immediately used in the organisation, it is more like research and development. The surveys are exchanged between these two processes, and there is a similar exchange with account definition. The outcome of the first two activities, such as the SWOT analysis, provides input for the service delivery definition process. This process also provides the general objectives and strategy for the last two activities in skills definition.

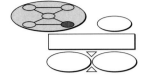

9.5 Technology definition

Objective
Technical developments are an important issue when determining the future of the services provided by the application management organisation. Technology is rapidly changing and as appropriate technical support is essential to application management, the choice of instruments is equally important. Technology definition is the process of selecting the instruments which the organisation will use to provide the services in the future.

Issues
We cannot support all technology
As an organisation cannot support all forms of technology we have to select the application management instruments. In this process we select development tools and future technology for application management and enhancement, such as ERP, VAG, Oracle, Visual Basic, XML, etc.

We often need more forms of technology and expertise than the organisation can cope with. In that case we need to select partners, in the market definition process. Hence, there are links between the market definition and technology definition processes.

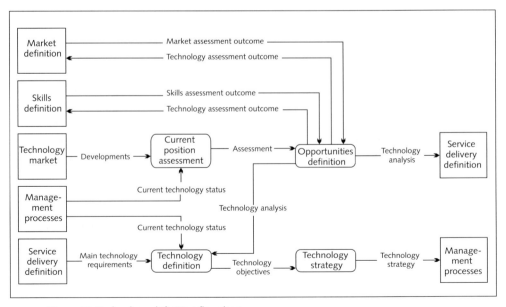

Figure 64 Technology definition flowchart

Activities
Survey of the current positions:
- defining the state of the art with respect to technical developments on the market;
- determining the continuity of the current tools and future options;
- determining additional technology requirements (e.g. the need for cost reduction or flexibility).

Identification of threats and opportunities:
- threats related to current technology and services;
- opportunities provided to the organisation by new technology.

Technology definition:
- definition and detailed development of the technology and infrastructure to be used in the long-term.

Strategy definition:
- determining the steps to acquire this technology and develop relevant expertise;
- determining the steps to be taken with respect to suppliers;
- determining the required relationship with suppliers (strategic partnerships, etc.).

Results
Technology assessment:
- survey of technology and developments;
- threats and opportunities.

Technology strategy:
- objectives with respect to technology;
- measures to investigate and select technology and incorporate it in the current quality system where relevant;
- potential technology partners.

Relationships
Management processes
Technology definition has a particularly close relationship with the quality management process which maintains the current quality system (including the application management infrastructure). The technology strategy is a primary input for quality management. Technology definition also has links with planning and control (capacity for investigation, testing and introduction) and cost management (in view of the cost of the technology).

OCM processes
The technology definition process has a close relationship with skills definition. The surveys and assessments are exchanged between these two processes. Technology definition

has a similar relationship with market definition. Finally, like the other OCM processes, it has links with service delivery definition.

ACM processes
There is no direct relationship with the ACM processes (which relate to the customer's information management) but it is advisable to be familiar with the outcome of the ICT developments strategy and other relevant issues.

9.6 Service delivery definition

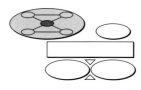

Objective
Service delivery definition is the process which identifies supply and demand and uses this information to set a strategy for the future. The objective of the process is to define the services to be provided in two or three years. The opportunities and restrictions associated with the current situation (market, accounts, skills, technology) are analysed and used to draw up a coherent policy which is then developed in greater detail in the other OCM processes.

Issues
Bottom-up first
According to the ASL philosophy, the best way to define the desired services is to start with a bottom-up approach, followed by a top-down approach. Through the other OCM processes we start by identifying developments, strengths and weaknesses, etc. related to the market, customers, technology and skills. This involves questions such as "What are we doing now, and how? What do our customers think about us? What developments are happening on the market?"

And then top-down
This information can be used to develop an image of what the application management organisation wants to be, where and why. This image or mission provides the starting point for the top-down development.

One option is to use the following list, but any other suitable method could be used:
- defining a mission: a short statement about the services to be provided in two to three years, the expertise they are based on, and the customer group they are offered to;
- defining objectives to realise the mission in verifiable units;
- defining one or more strategies to reach the defined objectives;
- identifying key success factors of the strategy;
- estimating and allocating the resources for the realisation;
- planning and scheduling the realisation objectives.

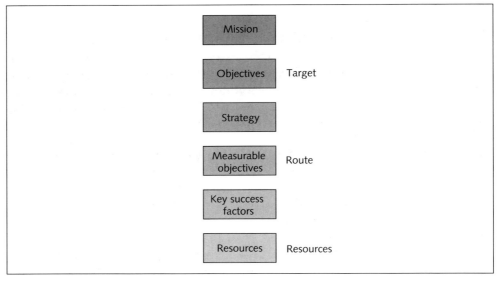

Figure 65 Policy model

In service delivery definition, the entire market, customers, skills and technology are relevant when developing the mission and taking decisions, and this is where the integration is provided. This defines:
- *what* services will be provided;
- *who* to;
- *how* they will be realised (e.g. make or buy);
- with what *resources* or development tools (e.g. ABAP and SAP);
- and what primary *skills* will be needed.

Detailed development
The detailed development of the strategy, e.g. with respect to the skills, occurs in the surrounding OCM processes (here: skills definition).

Activities
Defining the mission and objectives:
- defining the service catalogue in two or three years;
- defining the customers for these services in two or three years;
- defining the skills and expertise (capabilities) for these services and customers in two or three years.

Determining the strategy and route:
- determining outlines of the strategy to reach the objective;
- defining measurable objectives.

Chapter 9 Organisation Cycle Management

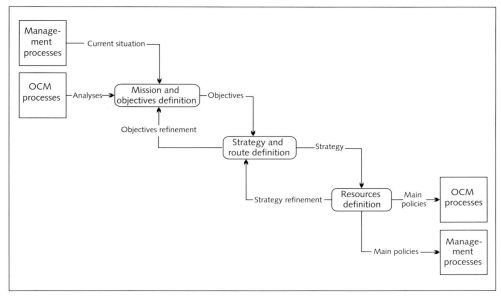

Figure 66 Service delivery definition flowchart

Determining the resources:
- determining the availability of the resources;
- determining the required resources;
- allocating the resources.

Results
Overall strategic plan:
- mission;
- service outlines: type of services, customer groups, skills;
- strategy and measures;
- resources: projects to be initiated, capacity/resources to be deployed.

Relationships
Other OCM processes
All other OCM processes provide surveys or overviews as input for the service delivery definition process. The overall outlines and objectives set out in the service delivery definition are then developed in detail in these other processes.

Management processes
The objectives and strategy set the course for all management processes.

CHAPTER 10

Relationships with other forms of management

The ASL messages
— Users and organisations need a single point of contact (interface) for ICT services.
— There are fundamental differences between the different forms of management (functional, technical and application management), and there are n-to-m relationships between them. This is why ASL only covers application management. A comprehensive process which covers functional, technical and application management often leads to unwieldy organisations and processes.
— The service team is the single point of contact. The service team puts the underlying services together.

10.1 Introduction

As discussed earlier, application management is one of the three forms of management. This leads to the following questions:
- Why is there not one, unified management model?
- How are the integrated services provided?
- How is this accomplished within the ASL framework?

All these questions are addressed in this chapter.

10.2 Why have ASL in addition to the other management models?

The different types of management were discussed in the introduction of this book, and it was explained that ASL is purely concerned with application management. Here we will discuss why we only need a framework for application management, rather than an integrated model.

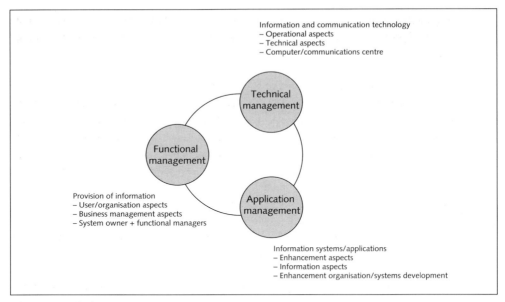

Figure 67 Forms of management

Relationships between different forms of management
ASL is not based on an integrated management model, and is indeed incompatible with that. The reasons for using ASL in addition to concepts such as ITIL are discussed below.

The different forms of management relate to different jobs and responsibilities
The different forms of management demand different approaches and expertise (see Figure 67). This is reflected in practice: in most cases, the different forms of management have different places in an organisation. The approaches are also different: application managers are primarily interested in the ease of enhancement, features or quality of an application. The business aspects are more distant to them. This is different for functional managers: they have a business focus and are primarily interested in the fit with the business process and costs. These forms of management are associated with different jobs and different, sometimes conflicting, approaches. These differences are resolved through negotiation. These negotiations have to be clearly defined, otherwise one of the approaches might be left out. The substantive differences, particularly between technical management and application management were already mentioned in the discussions of the management processes.

Flexibility requires the smallest possible units, not the largest possible ones
These forms of management are implemented separately by different organisations. Over time, these organisations change (outsourcing, decentralisation or centralisation, mergers or demergers). Not every organisation uses the same framework. It is easier to

separate the forms of management, so that not every change to the organisation rearranges all processes (in most cases, the change will be limited to one of the three management areas).

There is often no one-to-one relationship between the forms of management
Not every organisation includes all three forms of management. For example, small and medium-sized businesses do little in terms of application maintenance and enhancement. However, they do have technical management. Example: an application management organisation which supplies packages, has few operational relationships with technical management. Thus, a process model which covers all forms of management might include processes which are not actually present in the management organisation. In that case, it is difficult to define the process responsibility.

In fact, technical management is often concerned with many applications from different suppliers and sometimes even different service organisations. Large IT companies such as PinkRoccade and Getronics that provide technical management services have customers in many different organisations. Economies of scale are important to computer centres. Application management often provides applications (e.g. package suppliers) which run on different platforms, in many different organisations with separate computer centres. Functional management often uses a number of suppliers. Thus, there are no one-to-one relationships between these management organisations. Consequently, there cannot be a single process with one process owner which spans all forms of management. These complex process arrangements do not fit into a single process model, and similarly the process models cannot be easily covered by one organisation (unless the processes are separated again, as in ASL)

Separating responsibilities
Functional management essentially operates as the customer and application management and technical management as contractors. Defining one process with a single owner spanning these forms of management results in an undesirable situation: it is almost impossible to separate the customer from the contractor, and this leads to the past practice of the IT organisation telling the customer organisation what is going to happen.

Conditions for effective interfaces
This does not mean that these forms of management are not related. In fact, seamless support demands that these processes have effective interfaces. In fact, separating these forms of management (and ensuring good process interfaces between different forms of management) will result in flexible services which are easier to manage. However, this imposes some conditions on the way the processes are structured:
- Clear interfaces: there have to be unified process interfaces between the different forms of management (functional, application and technical management). Often, the activities will require information from another form of management.

- Agreements about the interfaces: not only should the interfaces be clearly defined, but quality criteria should also be defined, both relating to the product (what is supplied) and the process (who does what). Such agreements ensure that all three forms of management are accountable and manageable.
- Interface with other management models: this requires that the ASL framework is effectively connected with the other management models. This link has already been created to ITIL (infrastructure management) and FBM (functional management).

10.3 Process interfaces

The reasons for not integrating functional, technical and application management in a single process were discussed above. Here we will discuss the process structure and relationships between the three forms of management and the way they are arranged.

Role of functional management
The role of functional management is essential when setting up these processes. Functional management covers two areas:
- Setting a strategy for the standard infrastructure and its support. This refers to generic elements such as office automation and standard software such as word processing programs, spreadsheets, etc.
- Functional management is also responsible for the functionality of the applications. These applications run on the underlying infrastructure which functional management has little information about.

There is normally little overlap between the relevant flows of information and operations. Most of the changes in office automation, such as ordering another PC or an additional software package for a PC has little to do with the maintenance and enhancement of the business applications of an organisation. Most of the changes in applications have little or no impact on the office automation or infrastructure, particularly in large organisations. Furthermore, in technical management there tends to be a separation between office automation (often local) and the larger infrastructure (computer centre). This makes it possible to separate the management processes. The first group of activities are outside the scope of this book on application management.

Service and change
The earlier distinction between the roles of service provider and application innovator can also be interpreted more broadly, in terms of the other forms of management (i.e. functional management and technical management).

Service processes
We also find service processes in functional management. Examples include incident management, continuity management and capacity management. These processes can also be identified within technical management. Thus, there is a degree of commonality of these processes between the forms of management, but the substantive development of the processes will be different.

Innovative processes
Like application management, functional management includes innovative processes. These aim to improve the provision of information within the organisation, and to identify the necessary functions and requirements. This demands an understanding of the business processes and the user organisation, as functional management has to translate the developments in the business processes and user organisation into wishes and requirements for the provision of information and applications. Thus, the approach is focussed on the business processes.

Technical management also includes activities which aim to update the infrastructure. Major infrastructure changes often affect the applications. The detailed development of the innovative processes is highly dependent on the form of management (technical, functional or application management).

Relationships
Normally, the service processes within functional, application and technical management cooperate quite closely, as do the innovative processes. This cooperation is outlined in Figure 68

Maintenance
Functional management also provides input for the infrastructure, particularly for office automation. For this reason the maintenance processes within functional management are closely linked to the maintenance processes in technical management.

The functional management maintenance processes (circles on the left) also interact closely with the maintenance processes in application management where the operation of the applications is concerned.

The same applies to the maintenance processes in application management and the corresponding processes in technical management. Technical management provides the infrastructure used by application management, and application management specifies how it is used.

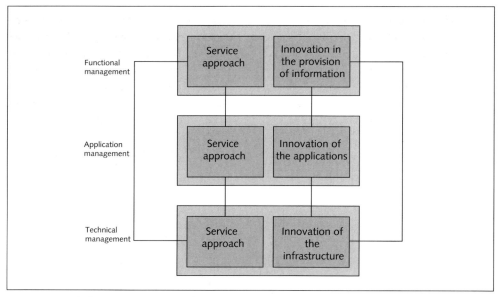

Figure 68 Relationships between the management models

> **Example**
> If recourse has to be made to an off-site back-up facility then application management will identify the minimum set of files and programs to be transferred. Technical management will provide the basic information (metrics) used for application management activities. In this case, technical management serves as a contractor (or sometimes subcontractor) to application management.

Innovation
The innovation processes in functional management also have close links with the processes in application management which are concerned with applications. Examples include defining the specifications of applications and undertaking acceptance tests. This makes functional management the primary point of contact for the ASL enhancement and renovation processes.

These relationships are not limited to the operational processes, as suggested by the examples above, but also occur in the strategic and management processes. Consequently, the detailed development of these relationships results in the slightly more complex figure below.

The main communication and management lines are shown in Figure 69, using application management and functional management as an example. The application management processes are placed in the lowest tier, and the functional management processes in the upper tier. The operational processes in application management are in the foreground and are closely linked to the operational processes in functional management (heavy lines). The integrated management within application management (represented by the block in the centre) has a similarly close relationship with the integrated management in functional management. The strategic innovation processes for the provision of information (ACM processes) are ideally undertaken by both application management and functional management in close cooperation.

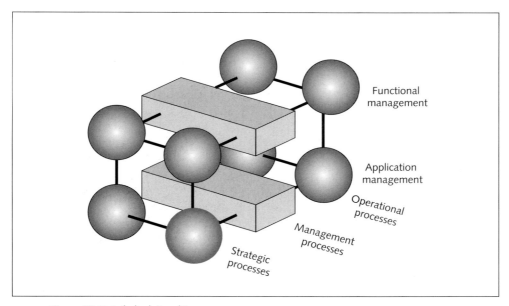

Figure 69 Detailed relationships

10.4 The service team and its structure

The process relationships between the different forms of management were discussed above. One of the objectives of ASL is to provide a clear interface and single point of contact to the users and customer, which is provided by the service team which is responsible for all IT services. In this way it implements the three different management processes.

What is the service team?

A service team forms a single point of contact for all organisations which provide the services. The service team is responsible for the implementation of both technical management and application management and represents the IT contractor. This means that the user organisation no longer needs to deal with a number of service contacts, or suffer from disputes between these contacts.

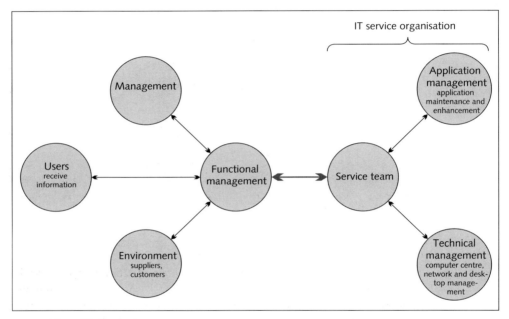

Figure 70 Service team

This means that the service team is the point of contact with functional management. The service team makes agreements about the services to be provided, stability in the future, availability, cost, periods, agreements and service levels.

The technical and application management processes come together in the service team. The service team is responsible for making the agreements with the parties which are needed to provide the whole range of services. The service team allocates issues to application management or technical management. Depending on the situation and the requirements, the service team will sometimes be primarily focussed on application management, and sometimes on technical management. Thus, this is where ITIL and ASL meet. The management processes play a key part in this.

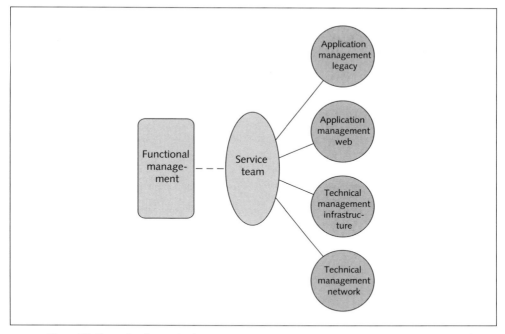

Figure 71 Example of a service team

Place of the service team in the overall structure
The service team often includes several organisations or organisation components who together provide the full range of services to the customer. The processes are combined in the service team. Cost management, service level management, quality management, and planning and control are combined. Conversely, if the flow is in the other direction, it is separated and allocated to the underlying processes. This means that the service team serves as the main contractor.

Criteria for setting up a service team
An effective service team has to fulfil a number of conditions and it should be productive. Relevant issues when setting up a service team include: who is the customer (who signs the contract), what services are provided, what options are there for providing integrated and cohesive services, are the cooperating or underlying parties prepared to offer services together, and are they prepared to follow this through?

Customer
An integrated service team which serves several customers (who either pay for it or are responsible for the budget) will normally only work with difficulty, particularly when application functions have to be requested. In the end, one party will have to be responsible for orders and agreements about the services to be obtained.

Uniform services

A service team and the processes can only be set up effectively if there are uniform services or a comprehensive range of services.

> **Example**
> The operation, maintenance and enhancement of a web-based system differs from the services required for legacy systems with strict security. Similarly, the requirements made of the processes are likely to be different. Web-based systems demand quick processes, and legacy systems need reliable specification and decision-making processes. Thus, if the processes for legacy and web-based systems are combined there will be conflicts, leading at best to a bland compromise. This means that these requirements and properties should be considered when setting up the processes. However, both may be covered by a single service team, although the underlying processes will be different.

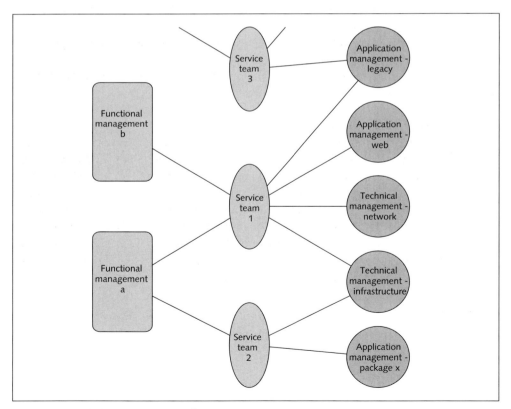

Figure 72 Service team network

If the services provided are not connected in any way then a service team will rarely be useful (there is not much synergy between a butcher and a furniture shop).

Uniform organisational structure
A service team will only be useful if there is a uniform organisational structure. This means that one party can operate as the main contractor, or several parties can operate together as the main contractor. The responsibilities, interests and management measures must be compatible. A service team which cannot enter into agreements on behalf of the underlying parties and which cannot solve the problems occurring between them simply isn't a service team.

Detailed structure
In the context of maintaining and enhancing applications it could happen that the user organisation does not have direct control over application management. This could happen if standard packages or ASP are used. In those cases the users rarely have direct control of the functions available. The opposite is bespoke software, or customised or modified packages, which are common with ERP software. In that case, functional management can control application management and make them responsible for processing operations, and there will be two options:
- application management forms the primary contact for the maintenance, enhancement and operation of the services;
- if there is no direct control of application management, then technical management will form the primary contact.

Application management as the primary contact
In this case, application management acts as a partner of functional management, and technical management is the subcontractor for the application operations. This approach is preferable as it provides functional management with a contact which is familiar with the business processes and can directly translate them into technical concepts. It is appropriate when bespoke software and customised packages are used. In this case, the maintenance processes of application management can serve as tier one with respect to functional management for the provision of application services. However, any technical management problems will also be application management problems. Consequently, the technical management interests are important.

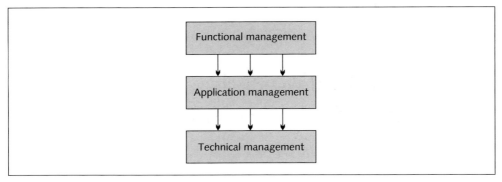

Figure 73 Application control, version 1

Technical management as the primary contact
In other cases, when the application management organisation is more remote, this function will have to be performed by technical management. Here, the technical management maintenance organisation will contact the application manager if there are any problems. The request will be addressed to the incident management desk of the application management organisation who will allocate somebody to provide assistance, depending on the agreements. A disadvantage of this arrangement is that the communications and problem resolution now include more steps and it will take longer to provide a solution. This approach is appropriate for packages and other standard software.

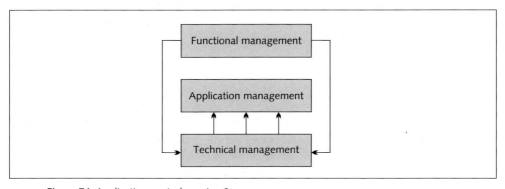

Figure 74 Application control, version 2

Summary
As discussed above, it is not possible to develop a standard model for the service team. This team should be set up to reflect the relevant situation and lines of management and control. ASL provides the building blocks which can be used in the context of functional management and ITIL. The ASL clusters are easily interfaced with other clusters.

CHAPTER 11

Application and introduction of ASL

The ASL messages
— ASL is a tool, not the central issue. "Because ASL requires it" is never a valid argument.
— There is no uniform method – it will be different in each case. Practical requirements form the initial input when setting up the processes. The best practices can help with their detailed definition. Modifying these best practices can lead to better practices.
— It is better to take just two modest steps forward than fail to reach the ideal situation (the best can get in the way of an improvement on the current situation). Trying to do too much at once is the major pitfall when making the operations more professional or improving quality. ASL assumes growth and improvement in steps.
— An organisation is never complete, its development has to continue, in-line with any problems experienced. This development may well include retracing your steps.

Much can be written about the introduction and application of ASL. There are plenty of pitfalls, and it would be impossible to describe them all. However, we will identify some of the major issues in this chapter, as they are inherent to ASL.

The advice in the messages above covers the following subjects:
- using ASL as a framework;
- the initial state of the organisation from which everything starts;
- the improvement process;
- the outcome of the improvement process.

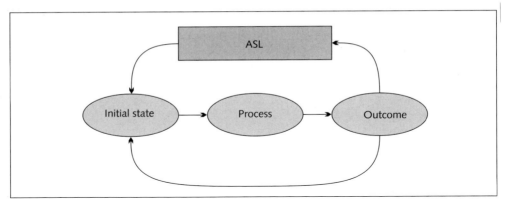

Figure 75 Improvement process

11.1 Applying the ASL framework

It's not about ASL, but about the best practices
ASL is a framework for application management. It is a process-based outline for the activities associated with the management, maintenance and enhancement of information systems. It provides a comprehensive check list of activities based on the experience of many professionals and organisations. ASL is based on a process model, i.e. a model of the processes used in application management. A process model is a simplification of the real world, and the process model in this book is simplified even more. This means that ASL does not provide rigid guidelines or required methods. It is a supporting tool for developing application management processes, and it is supplemented by best practices. In other words, it is rather like a check list.

Discussions about models always address the wrong subject
A model or framework always leads to discussions: something is missing from it, some processes will not work in the e-society or small-scale environments, or it does not cover something, etc. Discussions such as these are often unproductive. They are rather like the discussions of twenty years ago about the best methods for systems development. After a decade of discussions almost everybody agreed that the details of the method are not actually that important. The professional skills of the person implementing them are at least as important.

It is all a matter of seeing, being prepared to look, and being able to cope with limitations. In our experience, the ASL framework does cover all aspects of application management. However, in some environments the emphasis will be different. Instead of focussing on the differences, it would be more productive to look at the similarities. There will never be an ideal framework – what is ideal to one person may be wrong to the next.

Discussions about this can waste a lot of time, time which could have been used to take the organisation a step further. Anyway, ASL is an open framework and it is in the public domain – it can be modified. So you are free to improve it and we would encourage you to do so!

11.2 Initial state

Situations
Every organisation, every system, every user organisation is different. That is irrelevant to ASL: the best practices translate the framework to the situation at hand. For this reason, generic application management aspects were included in the ASL framework, while specific aspects are covered by the best practices. Different situations can lead to different implementations. Large and critical legacy systems usually have to be extremely reliable, transparent and effective. Consequently, the application management organisation will focus on the maintenance processes. These systems are often relatively stable which means that although the strategy processes are just as important, the do not have to be carried out that frequently. A rapid response will be much more important when dealing with communications and Internet-based systems. It is still advisable to use the maintenance and enhancement processes these environments, but they need not be as detailed, as the technology may have changed completely in three years' time. When introducing ASL, these choices and considerations are essential to a successful implementation. In most cases, there will be conflicts between cost-effectiveness, quality and flexibility.

11.3 Implementing ASL

Better one modest step forward than an unsuccessful jump
A great deal of experience has now been obtained with the improvement process. An ambitious start, a major commitment and theoretically well-developed with the objective of developing the perfect organisation. However, the real world is difficult. The vision behind ASL is more one of incremental improvement and growth. It is easier and better to make many small steps forward. In this way, the risk of failure is lower, people find it easier to adapt, and there is more time and space to make adjustments in the next step.

You have to know why
Normally, the reason for taking up the improvement process is that the current situation is not good enough and has to be improved. however, we prefer an approach based on problems and issues. You have to know why something should be improved. That means identifying objectives and clearly-defined problems: "we occasionally lose source code",

"the acceptance tests show they actually wanted something different", "our managers don't really know what we are doing", "you're just told to get started and then the priorities change, and then you have to get back to it after four months". By tackling clear problems which people experience themselves, both management and personnel will be committed to doing something about it – and therefore the improvement process will be effective. This can be emphasised through the scans and self-evaluations which are used to identify the problems and ambitions.

Feasibility is more important than formal correctness
ASL provides a large framework, with many processes. This provides opportunities to detail lots of issues and to develop procedures and forms for them. But that is not the intention of ASL. Instead, ASL is a framework to work better and with greater awareness. A bird in the hand is worth two in the bush. It is better to have some activities which are supported and implemented, than to do everything by the book, but without real support. Many processes do not have to be introduced or developed as a real process. It may be enough simply to do something, without clearly defining everything. So there shouldn't be paperwork just for the sake of it.

People aren't stupid
The people who work in application management are highly educated, most have a higher vocational or academic qualification, and many have been working in the field for years. So, they are intelligent and have experience. That is something which is often forgotten when introducing new methods and during improvement processes. However, these people can make valuable contributions. Our experience is that people often know how the job should be done, but the real world sometimes gets in the way. The introduction can be facilitated by using their experience and ensuring that relevant personnel make a major contribution to outlining the new situation. It will also make it easier to enforce the new discipline as people will be committed to it.

11.4 The end result

... is something we never reach

As we mentioned earlier, people, organisations, environments and expectations all change. After a successful improvement process, the dissatisfaction of the customers and users will grow after two or three years. They have become accustomed to the results and can no longer imagine that it used to be different. And there are other problems. Furthermore, the method described above often leaves something out. So there is no end. Once something is finished, we can get on with the next step.

Adjustments and retracing our steps
Not every improvement is successful, some might even have a negative impact. In that case we have to make adjustments or even retrace our steps. In a situation like that, sticking to the new method will be highly counterproductive.

Developing a new structure can be painful
An over-the-top example: personnel were expected to be proactive and take the initiative. Once that happened the manager applied the brake: they were not expected to do or develop things themselves. When processes are set up, there will be things which are no longer permitted. Activities we all agree are undesirable, like quickly pushing something through or hiding issues. Both management and personnel have to be aware of this and act accordingly. If they fail to do so, the changes will be of little use.

Learning from our mistakes
A best practice is the result of the lessons learned. It takes less effective practices to point us to the best practices. In some cases the experience is worth sharing with others – and you have the opportunity to do so, as you too can contribute best practices to ASL.

APPENDIX 1
ASL processes

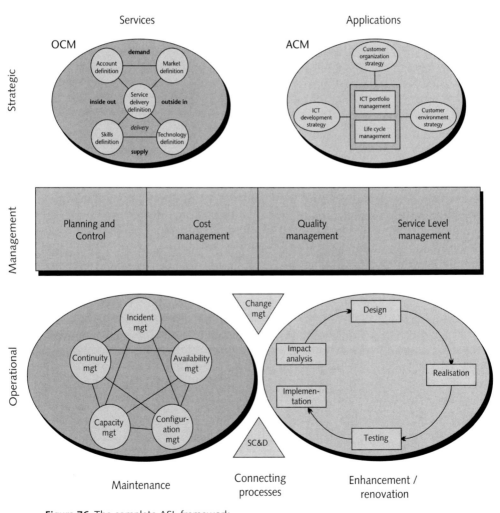

Figure 76 The complete ASL framework

APPENDIX 2

Notes to the process flowcharts

Process model
This discussion of the process model is primarily intended for readers with an interest in the theoretical aspects. The process descriptions are accompanied by flowcharts to support the text. These flowcharts are a theoretical presentation of the flows of information between the processes. This process model provides the foundation for the ASL framework.

Symbols
The flowcharts are actually data flow diagrams (DFD), which include four object types.

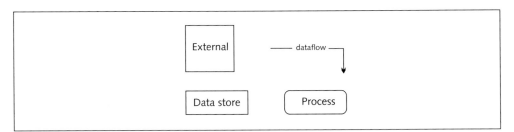

Figure 77 Flowchart symbols

DFD objects:
- Data stores: data storage media.
- Processes: activities which process information. A process can be defined into greater detail by decomposition into the underlying processes.
- Externals (or external entities): external recipients or producers of data.
- Data flows: flows of information between processes, data stores and externals.

Notes to the flowcharts
Close study of the flowcharts might suggest some apparent inconsistencies between them. This is because several processes such as configuration management, software

control and distribution, and change management provide information to many processes. To make the flowcharts less cluttered these data flows were not included. The same applies to the management processes within the operational processes. Furthermore, the flows within some processes are based on a generic model, for example those related to software control and distribution. This process issues and receives application objects. In the design process the received object is more specifically defined as 'approved specifications'.

The management processes are generic across all operational processes. Similarly, the strategic processes (ACM and OCM) are generic to all management processes. This means that these processes have data flows to or from the processes at the next lower level. For example, the output of all management processes to the operational processes is combined in data flows such as "planning, service levels, quality criteria, etc.". The output of these processes provides input to the management processes and is also modelled in generic terms.

Description of the process model
Some relatively complex modelling decisions were taken to make the flowcharts less cluttered. These decisions are based on the ASL objectives. For example each management process monitors the operational processes from a different angle (quality, service levels, etc.). The overall process model and all design decisions are described in the report 'Procesmodel ASL' (in Dutch). However, this is of limited value for the routine use of ASL.

APPENDIX 3

Further reading

The following publications address issues raised in this book:

Hinley, David S., *Content Design Barracuda, a methodology for the provision of Application Services*, PinkRoccade, 2000, Voorburg.
Pols, R. van der, *Procesmodel ASL*, internal report, PinkRoccade Atribit, 2000 (in Dutch).
Porter, M. E., *Competitive Advantage*, The Free Press, New York, 1985.
Yourdon, E., *Modern Structured Analysis*, Prentice Hall, 1989.
Zee, H. van der, P. van Wijngaarden, *Strategic Sourcing and Partnerships*, Addison Wesley Longman Nederland bv, Amsterdam, 1999.

APPENDIX 4

ASL Foundation

The ASL Foundation was set up in 2002 by a number of vendors and end users who wanted to raise Application Management to a higher professional level. The Foundation has adopted ASL, Application Services Library, as the standard for Application Management processes.

The Foundation gives professionals who want to improve methods and exchange best practices an opportunity to meet. This cooperation has many benefits as you will be able to improve you work processes on the basis of the experience of others, and vice versa. This will reduce costs and improve the services.

Activities

The Foundation undertakes the following activities:

Best Practices
The participating organisations have committed themselves to contribute best practices. Other organisations can also submit best practices. The Foundation reviews the quality of the proposed best practices and approved best practices are then published on the web site.

Training & Certification
Training personnel in Application Management is essential to ensure consistent terminology. The Foundation ensures that the modules offered by various training organisations are compatible. Training organisations can also apply for accreditation. The exams are organised by Exin, an independent organisation. The quality of the Application Management processes in an IT organisation can be certified by independent auditors.

Development
The Application Services Library is developing continuously and new contributions are always welcome. The Foundation compiles the contributions and helps to improve the ASL framework by organising themed meetings, discussion groups, etc.

Publicity
Effective publicity is one of the key factors in ensuring the adoption of ASL as the standard for Application Management processes. The Foundation publishes articles and books, organises seminars and presents ASL at network meetings and at interested organisations. Most of these activities are free of charge. All publications and standard presentations can be downloaded from the web site www.aslfoundation.org or ordered on info@aslfoundation.org.

Participation

If you are interested in this new standard and want to help improve the quality of application management you can participate in one of three ways:

Individual
As an individual participant you can join the activities and you will have the access to the knowledge network of the Foundation.

Knowledge partner
All employees of your organisation or business unit will have the same benefits, in your country, as individual participants. Your company name will be mentioned in presentations and on the web site and reciprocal links can be set up.

Participant
Participants form the governing body of the Foundation and are committed to providing the human resources to realise the Foundation targets. They are at the heart of the Foundation on an international scale. Participants are directly associated with the goal of the Foundation: professional application management.

For more information visit www.aslfoundation.org or mail on info@aslfoundation.org.